INSIGHT GUIDES

ORLANDO
smart guide

APA PUBLICATIONS L
Part of the Langenscheidt Publishing Group

Contents

Below: astronauts preparing for launch.

Left: Disney's iconic castle dominates the Magic Kingdom.

Atlas

Below: a rare chance to meet a star.

3

Orlando

Not many destinations promise to take you to the "Happiest Place on Earth". Cynics might argue Orlando should not promise this either, but there is no denying that this modern city in the heart of sub-tropical Floridia has become a tourist mecca, not for its natural wildlife and agreeable climate, which it has in abundance, but because of one pair of ears, recognized the world over.

Destination Facts and Figures

Size of Walt Disney World Resort: **47sq miles**
Number of hotel rooms in Orlando: **115,200**
Number of restaurants in Orlando: **5,390**
Orlando's total shopping space: **52 million sq ft**
Number of residents in Greater Orlando: **1.9 million**
Number of visitors to Orlando each year: **49 million**
Economic impact of visitors: **$29.6 billion**
Cost of land purchased by Walt Disney for his resort: **$5 million**
Number of public or semi-private golf courses: **176**
Ratio oak trees to residents in Winter Park: **3:4**
The first African-American township in America: **Eatonville, near Maitland**

The Land Built for a Mouse

Even before Disney's unique brand of entertainment arrived, the climate and savage beauty of Florida's landscape were attracting over 50,000 visitors each year – and that was in the 1870s. Roughly 100 years later Walt Disney's dreamlands arrived and everything about central Florida changed. Swamplands were reclaimed for theme parks, identikit holiday homes were built with alligator fences to protect their private pools, the cattle and citrus industries that had for so long dominated the state's economy were quickly forced into the backseat with tourism driving development, and the heart of Orlando began its never-ending battle with the whims of Disney.

For most youngsters and even some oldsters, Disney is synonymous with a dream vacation. This is not just because of a price that forces people into months, if not years, of planning and saving; but because of the childhood dreams that Disney promises to fulfill. When a little girl meets Snow White or a boy shakes the hand of Peter Pan it is a dream that has come true and who could begrudge a young child for calling this moment "magical."

Although not cheap by any means, a Disney vacation may be better value than you imagine. By the time you've checked out of a well-appointed Disney Resort, having been consistently greeted with a smile and had constant entertainment for your children, you may find you've bagged a bargain. The Disney experience is so unique that any price seems a steal. Added into this value is that everything at Disney, from cleaning maids to Cinderella's smile, works like clockwork thanks to a terrifyingly efficient management structure that seems capable of eliminating all potential problems. This may not really be the "Happiest Place on Earth", but it is not from lack of trying.

Imaginary Lands and Tourist Traps

Disney's draw knows no socio-economic bounds and for those unwilling to pay inflated resort prices, there are countless places to eat, sleep, and play along International Drive

Below: often overlooked by tourists, Downtown Orlando has a thriving art and nightlife scene.

and US192 that offer discounted deals and cheap thrills in an effort to entice the weary hordes away from the all-inclusive resorts.

Some attractions such as Universal Resorts and SeaWorld can compete with The Mouse, others are poor imitations. Hotels may offer more family-friendly options at better prices than Disney, while other cheap stays are shabby beyond repair, and for every fine restaurant there are at least two poor fast-food outlets looking to make a quick buck. The gaudiness of these off-resort areas should be experienced, if only to increase your appreciation of the well-designed theme parks; but be wary. For some businesses, once proximity to Disney is secured, emphasis on quality of service or goods receives little attention.

The Cultural Heart: Downtown and Winter Park

This makes it such a pity that the distance to Orlando's "real life" is so great. Downtown Orlando is an important business center with a budding nightlife and arts scene. Winter Park, home of Rollins College, is rich in culture and has fantastic shopping, gourmet dining, and European-style cafés.

Don't let these gems go overlooked. Disney may go to any length to appeal to the child inside, but these real, functioning communities offer the indulgences of a grown-up vacation.

Highlights

▲ **Epcot's** famous sphere marks the entrance to a park revealing technological wonders and cultures from around the globe.
▶ Real wildlife and models of dinosaurs dominate the attractions at the **Animal Kingdom**.

▶ **Sea World** provides an opportunity to interact with sea animals, such as dolphins, penguins, and killer whales.

▲ The 16 **thrill rides** of Orlando's theme parks, especially Islands of Adventure, attract adrenaline junkies from around the world.

▲ Kids can't get enough of the **Magic Kingdom's** characters and attractions.
▶ Visiting the **Kennedy Space Center** is a true once in a lifetime opportunity.

The Magic Kingdom

For most visitors the charming, child-friendly Magic Kingdom is synonymous with Disney World. This was the resort's original park and is still its best. For younger children the chance to meet Cinderella or Peter Pan really is a dream come true, and many of the slow, dark rides here are perfectly weighted to spark their imagination without igniting fear. Some teenagers may find this park a bit too "kiddy," but there is no shortage of adults fulfilling long-held childhood dreams by shaking Mickey's hand or wearing a pair of ears all day long. It's hard not to admire the attention to detail, and the fireworks show that ends each day is superb.

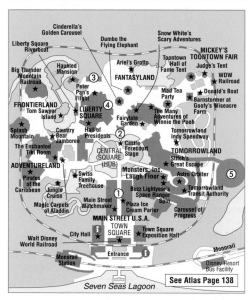

See Atlas Page 138

Seven Seas Lagoon

If you are not staying at a Disney Resort, allow plenty of time to get to and from your car to the park entrance. Trams from the parking lot drop guests off at the Ticket and Transportation Center, where you can buy your ticket and then board a boat or the monorail to reach the main entrance. From here you join the other crowds that have been directly deposited from their Disney Resort transportation.

Town Square Exposition Hall. When not being used for conventions or presentations, the auditorium shows continuous reels of classic Disney films. This quiet and cool retreat on the fringes of the park is almost always empty.

Main Street, U.S.A.

The Magic Kingdom hits you the minute you walk through the gates. Music sets a dreamy tone, and suddenly the real world is replaced by an idealized version of a Victorian-era American small town – this is **Main Street, U.S.A.** ① Before you explore its collection of shops and attractions, use the practical facilities at **Town Square** to get yourself orientated.

The **City Hall** to the left of the park entrance has maps and information and can book meals. It also contains the park's lost and found office.

Above the park's entrance gates is one of the stations for the **Walt Disney World Railroad**, which also has stations in Frontierland and Mickey's Toontown Fair.

To the right of the main entrance is the tucked-away

Otherwise, Main Street is meant to be explored. In addition to the highly decorated souvenir shops there are such gems as the barber's shop with a barbershop quartet and the **Main Street Watchmaker**, which sells timepieces featuring Disney characters.

Of course, any visit to Main Street, U.S.A. would not be complete without dropping in to the **Plaza Ice Cream Parlor** for a sundae.
SEE ALSO SHOPPING, P.112

The Hub and Cinderella's Castle

The Magic Kingdom was designed in a hub-and-spoke style. At the end of Main Street, U.S.A. the hub connects four spokes to Adventureland, Liberty Square and Frontierland, Fantasyland and Mickey's Toontown Fair, and Tomorrowland. At the center of the connecting hub is **Cinderella's Castle** ②: its Forecourt Stage is home to **Dream Along with Mickey**, the park's newest live show.

Though the castle serves as the park's signature backdrop, inside there is only **Cinderella's Royal Table**, a sit-down restaurant that lets you dine with the entire gaggle of Disney princesses. Little girls and, let's face it, some fathers have dreamt of this opportunity for years.

SEE ALSO LIVE SHOWS, P.76; RESTAURANTS, P.98

Adventureland

There is more than a hint of Disney nostalgia at Adventureland. Many of its attractions, though updated, date from the Magic Kingdom's beginning and provide a unique insight into the early days of theme parks.

Jungle Cruise is the most charming of the early attractions. This light-hearted cruise through the jungle rivers of the world is frequently disrupted by attacks from disgruntled natives, crocs, hippos, and elephants.

Next door is the legendary **Pirates of the Caribbean**, which has the notoriety of being the only theme park ride later to become a movie. This dark ride has been frequently updated since its opening to conform to changing codes of decency, yet it still paints a colorful portrait of pirate life. Its most recent adaptation has seen the addition of an animatronic Captain Jack Sparrow

from the film, making Johnny Depp one of the few human film stars to feature in a Magic Kingdom ride.

The other attractions in Adventureland serve to entertain kids with time to spare. These include the **Magic Carpets of Aladdin**, a basic hub-and-spoke ride; the **Swiss Family Treehouse**, a free play area based on the Robinsons' fictional home; and **The Enchanted Tiki Room**, a short show featuring animatronic birds. It does provide a chance to cool off, if not much else.

Frontierland

The home of good ol' fashioned country living, Frontierland features characters such as Song of the South's Brer Rabbit and Tom Sawyer. It also has two of the park's thrill rides – **Splash Mountain** and **Big Thunder Mountain Railroad**. Though both rides are tame in comparison to other parks' roller coasters, they make a good stepping stone for children who have recently outgrown kiddie-coasters.

Tucked away in Frontierland's corner is **Tom Sawyer Island**, a free play area for children that includes rope

Above: familiar Disney characters from classic films and modern creations.

bridges to cross and caves and trails to explore.

Along the road to Liberty Square there are several shops and smaller attractions such as a shooting arcade. Also here is the **Country Bear Jamboree**, a stage show featuring animatronic bears leading children in songs.
SEE ALSO THRILL RIDES, P.124

Liberty Square

Sandwiched between Frontierland and Fantasyland, Liberty Square recreates a New England town center. In addition to the leisurely **Liberty Square Riverboat** ride along the Rivers of America, there is the **Hall of Presidents**. This patriotic attraction features every US president in animatronic form, with the current president leading the show.

Without a doubt the most enjoyable attraction on Liberty Square is the slightly scary **Haunted Mansion**. This more sophisticated dark ride explores a dusty old house in which holograms, lasers, and other special effects make ghosts appear all around you, even in your carriage.

Fantasyland

For most visitors under the age of ten Fantasyland could be a destination in itself. Cinderella's Castle creates the perfect backdrop, and every attraction celebrates a childhood favorite, from Mickey Mouse to Peter Pan.

One of the park's original attractions is **it's a small world** ③. This voyage through animatronic nations of the world is accompanied by a song that is sung in various languages throughout the boat ride, but sticks in everyone's head after they disembark. It's curious to see just how Disney saw the world in the late 1960s – a tableau of superficial stereotypes that today would shame any travel publication.

Across from here are two of Fantasyland's finest children's attractions.

Character greetings play a huge part of the experience at the Magic Kingdom and other theme parks. These occur in two different formats. The first is the regularly scheduled events, which you can find listed on your Times Guide. But unexpected appearances often occur, too, when anyone from the famous Cinderella to a recent unknown will appear in the park for a limited time to pose for pictures and sign autographs.

dren's attractions. **Peter Pan's Flight** is a fantastic dark ride over the streets of London to Neverland. Your pirate ship flies past key scenes from the classic Disney film before touching down. **Mickey's Philhar-Magic** ④ plays on vintage films, too, incorporating countless songs and characters into this 4-D movie aimed at younger children (most other 4-D films in Orlando are much too scary for the little ones).

Other attractions in Fantasyland include **Cinderella's Golden Carousel** and **Dumbo the Flying Elephant**, a hub-and-spoke ride that lifts riders in the air. Not to be missed is a ride on the dizzying tea-cups of the **Mad Tea Party** – a classic funfair ride. All three are good options when short waiting times are at a premium.

Fantasyland has two more slow rides aimed at children. **Snow White's Scary Adventures**, though recently toned down, may still be too intense for the youngest guests; meanwhile, **The Many Adventures of Winnie the Pooh** is a ride that is worth no one's time, as it feels in every way a poor imitation of the slow rides Disney normally does so well.

Quieter times are to be had at the **Fairytale Garden** between **Cinderella's Castle** and the entrance to Tomorrowland, where Belle from *Beauty and the Beast* tells stories; at **Ariel's Grotto**, home of the Little Mermaid; and at **Pooh's Playful Spot**, a playground for younger children.

Mickey's Toontown Fair

Mickey's Toontown Fair is the most recent addition to the Magic Kingdom and focuses squarely on young children, giving them a chance to meet characters, especially Mickey Mouse in the **Judge's Tent**. Little ones can also look through either Minnie or Mickey's house (despite their years together the royal couple still do not cohabitate).

Other characters greet children throughout the day at the **Toontown Hall of Fame Tent**. The only ride at the fair is the **Barnstormer at Goofy's Wiseacre Farm**, an introductory roller coaster with a height requirement of 35in. There is also a water playground called **Donald's Boat** and a station for the **Walt Disney World Railroad** that can take you straight back to the entrance or around the park to Frontierland.

Tomorrowland

Built to resemble a Jules Verne-esque world of the future, Tomorrowland now feels slightly faded, but is not without its charms. The biggest draw is **Space Mountain** ⑤, the Magic Kingdom's most intense thrill ride.

If you arrive at Tomorrowland from Fantasyland you will pass the noisy **Tomorrow-**

land Indy Speedway, a souped-up go-cart track that takes many of the controls out of the drivers' hands.

Tomorrowland has many smaller attractions to explore. The **Astro Orbiter** is a traditional hub-and-spoke ride that goes much higher than most. Also over-head is the **Tomorrowland Transit Authority**, a mini-monorail that circles the area with little drama.

Two dark alien adventures await. In **Buzz Lightyear's Space Ranger Spin**, you get the chance to shoot aliens with a ray gun from a spinning spaceship, while at **Stitch's Great Escape** (minimum height: 40in), a slightly scary teleport simulator tricks you into thinking that an alien has gotten loose in the room, and includes long periods of complete darkness.

The newest attraction is **Monsters, Inc. Laugh Floor**, an interactive show that lets guests submit jokes to be retold by the Monsters themselves.
SEE ALSO THRILL RIDES, P.124

Seeing It All

Though the Magic Kingdom stays open from 9am until late every day of the week, it is nearly impossible for a young family (this park's target market) to see it all in one day and still have the energy to enjoy the fantastic fireworks that end the day.

If you are staying nearby or at a Disney resort, the best approach for this park is to get here in time to see the whimsical opening ceremony and then head back to your hotel for lunchtime and a break. Come back around 4pm to finish the park. Though this will mean missing the afternoon **Disney Dreams Come True Parade**, it will allow you plenty of time to find a choice place for the much more elaborate **Spectro-Magic** parade and **Wishes**, the nighttime fireworks show. After a day this full, few will find it hard to get to sleep once they finally return to the hotel.
SEE ALSO LIVE SHOWS, P.76

The Magic Kingdom

Epcot

While the Magic Kingdom focuses on the child in us all, the two halves of Epcot appeal to a more mature palate. What began as Walt Disney's "Experimental Prototype Community of Tomorrow" has become one of Disney's most enigmatic parks. Its sprawling layout invites slow exploration and demands a lot of walking; the environmental messages of Futureworld are sponsored by corporations with less than green reputations; the fine ethnic cuisines served at World Showcase are surrounded by endless souvenir shops making a quick buck on global cultures. For many the enigma gives way to intrigue, making Epcot their best day out.

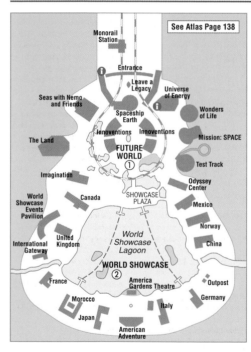

See Atlas Page 138

If you are staying at any of the Epcot resorts or coming from Hollywood Studios, you may find it easier to enter the park via boat at the International Gateway located between France and the United Kingdom: it's a smoother ride than the genuine English Channel.

resort's second theme park. Future World, anchored by Spaceship Earth, pays homage to Walt's original idea and is where the tour begins.

Future World ①

Beyond the entrance and below the orb of **Spaceship Earth** is the **Leave a Legacy** sculpture – plinths covered in steel etchings of past visitors. The Spaceship itself, forever the park's icon, is the home of **Project Tomorrow**, a slow ride that traces communication from Cro-Magnon man to the future. As is the case in many of Disney World's older attractions, the future is beginning to look a lot like the past.

UNIVERSE OF ENERGY

Turn to the left and you could find yourself confronted by **Universe of Energy**, spon-

The Disney Dream that Didn't Come True

When Walt Disney pitched the original Epcot in the 1970s, the "Experimental Prototype Community of Tomorrow" vision was of a controlled, planned community that showcased American innovation in technology and showed how its application could improve everyday life. Unlike modern America, this vision relied on public transportation and relegated cars underground. Unfortunately for green living, this vision died alongside Walt in 1966. In its place sprang Epcot, the

Left: Spaceship Earth.

slow, dark ride featuring characters from the *Finding Nemo* film. Once at Sea Base Alpha you have the chance to see all sorts of aquatic creatures, from clownfish to dolphins, and even humans participating in **DiveQuest**. Its **Coral Reef Restaurant** is one of the finest dining experiences this side of Showcase Lagoon.

SEE ALSO BEHIND THE SCENES, P.54–5; RESTAURANTS, P.99

THE LAND

The strongest environmental message in the whole park is sponsored by Nestlé and found inside **The Land** pavilion – if only an environmentalist's discomfort ended there. The Circle of Life features characters from *The Lion King* who are persuaded by Simba to stop the needless destruction of their native habitat for a useless holiday resort – a paradoxical sentiment for Disney to endorse by anyone's standards.

Living with the Land is an intriguing, slow boat ride through different exhibits about maximizing agricultural production without destroying natural habitat. Nothing wrong there, but when the "revolutionary" methods discussed include

sored by ExxonMobil. The only attraction here is **Ellen's Energy Adventure**. This positive spin on energy acquisition and production is easily the park's worst attraction; don't let it ruin the start to an intriguing park.

MISSION: SPACE AND TEST TRACK

Even more reason to move on is that next comes **Mission: SPACE**, the park's best thrill ride. There is a milder version now available for those who'd like to experience the visuals of lift-off without feeling the G-force. Either way you'll exit to the **Advanced Training Lab**, an intriguing interactive and play area.

Next door is the park's long-time favorite, **Test Track**. Sponsored by General Motors, this ride simulates the tests new cars endure before being cleared for safety.

SEE ALSO THRILL RIDES, P.124

In the center of the park there are Innoventions East and West, filled with interactive exhibitions showing off the latest in video games and robotics.

THE SEAS WITH NEMO AND FRIENDS

To the right of Spaceship Earth as you enter are three more pavilions. The **Seas with Nemo and Friends** is an enormous aquarium called Sea Base Alpha and reached via a Clam-mobile through a

Below: Mission: SPACE – G-forces await.

Left: looking at the lagoon from Japan.

Mayan temple. The only ride in Mexico is the **Gran Fiesta Tour Starring the Three Caballeros,** a poor dark ride featuring Donald Duck touring various Mexican landscapes.
SEE ALSO RESTAURANTS, P.100

NORWAY

The land of the Vikings is retold in **Maelstrom,** a slow boat ride with unexpected turns and drops that finishes with a short film about the Norwegian way of life. The main features of the pavilion are a recreated stave church and a Norwegian castle that houses the **Akershus Royal Banquet Hall.**
SEE ALSO RESTAURANTS, P.98

CHINA

China features one of the best shops in World Showcase, a fine restaurant in the **Nine Dragons,** and an enjoyable Circle-Vision (the screen wraps completely around the audience) film called *Reflections of China*. Set in a recreated temple, it takes you from the Great Wall of China to Hong Kong and shows some of the most remarkable natural environments, not just in China but the world.
SEE ALSO RESTAURANTS, P.99

GERMANY

There are no proper attractions at Germany, but with a year round *Oktoberfest* atmosphere and several fine German beers on offer, no one ever really seems to notice. The **Biergarten Restaurant** is the main attraction here, but shops in half-timber houses also sell some fine Christmas ornaments and quality wooden toys for younger children.
SEE ALSO RESTAURANTS, P.98

natural pest control and composting (techniques any hobby gardener could describe) one begins to fear the stewardship of commercial agriculture. You will see many of the crops grown here on the menu at the **Garden Grill**.

One unqualified success in The Land is **Soarin'** (minimum height: 40in) a hanggliding simulator that takes you over various sights of outstanding beauty in California.

IMAGINATION

The main attraction in this pavilion is **Honey, I Shrunk the Audience,** a 4-D movie based upon the *Honey, I Shrunk the Kids* movies. Older kids will enjoy the special effects here, but younger ones may be confused or terrified by the enormous 3-D dog trying to lick them.

Other attractions include **Journey into Imagination with Figment,** which starts out as a typical dark ride, but has periods of complete darkness and loud noises. **ImageWorks** is an interactive playground that uses various tricks of photography.

World Showcase ②

Some children may find World Showcase – a quick tour through 11 nations of the world – a bore, but most adults, at least those that like to shop, eat or drink, will love it. Each pavilion gives you the chance to experience a nation's consumables without actually visiting the country.

As this half of Epcot usually stays open later than Future World, a couple could easily make a romantic, if early, night of it here. In some ways it's even better than Downtown Disney as the food is more varied and the atmosphere, especially at night, less hectic.

MEXICO

Top of the romantic destination list would be the dimly lit **San Angel Inn Restaurante,** set under a recreated

Numerous live acts perform around Epcot daily, including the World Showcase Players (a drama group). More land-specific entertainment includes Mo'Rockin, Morocco's lively musicians; China's impressive Dragon Legend Acrobats; and the *lederhosen*-clad Oktoberfest Musikanten in Germany.

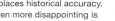

ITALY

Designer labels, fine wines, and even ashtrays are for sale in the Italy pavilion, which is a collage of Venetian architecture that includes the Doge's Palace and the Campanile from St Mark's Square. Italian cuisine is served up in **L'Originale Alfredo di Roma Ristorante**.

SEE ALSO RESTAURANTS, P.99

AMERICAN ADVENTURE

Portraying one's own country in a land of sweeping generalizations was always going to make interesting viewing for outsiders. No one will be surprised by the patriotic nature of the attractions, but the **Spirit of America Fife and Drum Corps**, the **Voices of Liberty**, and even the **American Adventure** film do their best to explain this patriotism to foreign guests. The film, which features an animatronic Ben Franklin and Mark Twain among others, does its best to provide a balanced view of American history by including the destruction of Native American culture and the horrors of slavery. By the end,

though, emotive patriotism replaces historical accuracy. Even more disappointing is that with America's rich culinary scope, from Cajun cornbread to New England clam chowder, Disney chose for the **Liberty Inn** to serve burgers and fries.

JAPAN

Just like the real country, many people could come to Japan just to shop. There is a huge selection of smartly designed sushi plates and knives, silk garments, eccentric toys, and other delicate trinkets. Though the quick-service restaurants here serve fine sushi, the **Teppanyaki Dining Rooms** is the best place for a sit-down meal.

SEE ALSO RESTAURANTS, P.100

MOROCCO

The Morocco pavilion has some of the finest faux architecture in World Showcase. You can even have a go at getting lost in the warren of shops selling Eastern art and dress, including fine rugs and bronzework. The country's cuisine is summed up at **Restaurant Marrakesh**.

SEE ALSO RESTAURANTS, P.100

FRANCE

It should be no surprise that you get two fine restaurants, **Chefs de France** and **Bistro de Paris**, and an accomplished patisserie in France. There is also a fine wine shop and, in the ultimate sign of good taste, a store selling Insight Guides. **Impressions de France** is a panoramic film shown throughout the day that takes you on a sweeping journey over the French countryside.

SEE ALSO RESTAURANTS, P.98–9

UNITED KINGDOM

Get your gourmandizing done before you leave France – fish and chips are the main fare in the UK. This little Britain has everything from Blighty, including a Beatles cover band at the Rose and Crown Pub (binge drinkers not supplied).

CANADA

America's neighbor gets a rugged interpretation with mountainous terrain and the Circle-Vision Film, *O Canada!* The signature restaurant **Le Cellier Steakhouse** serves meals hearty enough for any lumberjack.

SEE ALSO RESTAURANTS, P.99

SEEING IT ALL

If you are a quick walker you can see all of Epcot in one day, albeit a very long one. Though the distances to be covered are vast, the park has less time spent waiting for rides than others, as much of World Showcase can be seen at your own pace. Do make reservations if you have your heart set on a particular restaurant, as tables fill quickly.

Left: a great imitation of Venetian landmarks.

Animal Kingdom

For nearly 30 years Disney World believed animatronic animals were a more easily maintained attraction than their real counterparts, but then success at SeaWorld and Busch Gardens showed the value of genuine wildlife. In 1998 Disney opened the Animal Kingdom – a well-designed zoo loaded with big attractions. While animals and conservation are the main themes in areas such as Rafiki's Planet Watch, Discovery Island, and Oasis, they are quickly brushed aside in other areas, letting themed dinosaur digs, the new Expedition Everest thrill ride, and live shows like the Festival of the Lion King entertain the kids.

Seeing it Slowly

The crowds filing through **Oasis**, and youngsters driving parents on, mean few guests take time to appreciate the exhibitions here, which include everything from jewel-blue macaws to snuffling warthogs.

This is why the Animal Kingdom should be savored slowly. When watched patiently, animals do the darnedest things. Spending even two full days here is barely enough time to appreciate the park in full.

The **Rainforest Café** is one of only two table-service restaurants in the park.
SEE ALSO RESTAURANTS, P.100

See Atlas Page 138

RAFIKI'S PLANET WATCH ★ Affection Section
Conservation Station
Safari Area
Habitat Habit!
Wildlife Express Train
AFRICA
Maharajah Jungle Trek ★ ASIA
Pangani Forest Exploration Trail ★
Anandapur
Wildlife Express Train ③
Harambe ★ Flights of Wonder
Dawa Bar ★ Kali River Rapids ★
DISCOVERY ISLAND ① Discovery River ④
Discovery Island Trails ★ It's Tough to be a Bug ★ The Boneyard ⑥
Greeting Trails ★ TriceraTop ★ ★ Primeval Whirl
The Oasis Spin DINOLAND U.S.A.
② CAMP MINNIE MICKEY Entrance Dino-Sue ★ ⑤
Pocahontas and Her Forest Friends ★
Rainforest Cafe
Disney Resort Bus Facility P

Discovery Island ①

Discovery Island is the hub of the park, with the 14-story artificial banyan tree, called the **Tree of Life**, providing orientation for guests. The **Discovery Island Trails** are meandering walks punctuated by unique creatures in artificial habitats.

The main reason people come to Discovery Island, other than to cross to a new land, is to see the 4-D show, **It's Tough to be a Bug**, based on the film, *A Bug's Life* and starring the same creatures. Older kids will find the special effects amusing, but under-8s may find the unexpected smells, sprays, and sensations a bit too lifelike.

As the island is at the center of things, there are several cafeteria-style restaurants here where you can grab a bite, and several standard souvenir shops where you can spend a buck.

Camp Minnie Mickey

This land features the park's best live show, **Festival of the Lion King ②**, and the conservation-minded **Pocahontas and Her Forest Friends**. The former should not be missed, while the latter serves little purpose other than to get off your feet.

Left: close encounters.

guaranteed to get you wet, whether you like it or not.

Like the Pangani Forest Trail, the **Maharajah Jungle Trek** is a walk through traditional, though highly themed, zoo enclosures. It's your chance to see tapirs, Komodo dragons, and tigers living amid ancient palace ruins. **Flights of Wonder** is a chance to get out of the sun to see some birdlife do amazing tricks.
SEE ALSO LIVE SHOWS, P.78; THRILL RIDES, P.125

DinoLand U.S.A.

DinoLand U.S.A. creates a fairground atmosphere with traditional games you can pay to play. **TriceraTop Spin** is a traditional hub-and-spoke ride, while **Primeval Whirl** is an old-timey-looking roller coaster with a twist: the car spins as you go.

While kids love to play in **The Boneyard**, a playground that recreates a dinosaur dig, most adults never have either to ride **DINOSAUR** ⑤, a thrilling dark ride that takes you back in time to capture DNA from the last remaining dinosaur on the planet, or to spend their spare time while waiting to see **Finding Nemo – the Musical** ⑥.
SEE ALSO LIVE SHOWS, P.77

The **Greeting Trails** are the area's other attraction. The characters change throughout the day and the lines can get long, but it is a handy way to kill time while waiting to see the Festival of the Lion King.
SEE ALSO LIVE SHOWS, P.77–8

Africa

Kilimanjaro Safaris ③ is the main attraction in the recreated African town of Harambe. This ride showcases Disney's clever design skills that make the barriers between you and the giraffes, elephants, and rhinos invisible – an attempt to create a genuine safari experience; the ride is bumpy once the poachers get involved.

The **Pangani Forest Exploration Trail** is a more traditional zoo experience, with reinforced glass protecting you from the many gorillas and other animals. Not to be missed is the underwater hippo-viewing pool. This enormous creature is absolutely amazing to see as it swims past viewers.

Rafiki's Planet Watch

From Africa you can board a train to Rafiki's Planet Watch. This mini-land has interactive exhibits that focus on animal conservation and teach you how to encourage wildlife to live in your garden back home. There is also a petting zoo called **Affection Section**.

Asia

Thrill rides dominate Anandapur, Disney's collage of the Indian subcontinent. The big attraction is **Expedition Everest** ④, Disney World's newest roller coaster. **Kali River Rapids** is a much tamer affair, but this whitewater ride is

Kodak estimates that roughly 4 percent of all the amateur photographs taken in the US are snapped at either Walt Disney World or Disneyland.

Below: Kilimanjaro Safaris.

Hollywood Studios

It is no coincidence that Hollywood Studios opened the same year as Universal Studios. Disney believes strongly in giving competition to the competition. What makes Hollywood Studios more attractive to most guests, other than it being handily located on the Disney World Resort, is its more child-friendly nature and Disney's faultless "imagineering." Though it is hardly the resort's most successful park, it provides behind-the-scenes access to not just loud and flashy film stunts, but to quiet, retiring animators, too. And there are thrill rides here that not even a grumpy teenager could call lame. An extra bonus is that you can easily see it all in one day.

Hollywood Boulevard

Just past Hollywood Studio's Art Deco entrance gates you enter a square, the beginning of Hollywood Boulevard, with facilities to help you get oriented and one of the best shops in the entire Disney World Resort, **Sid**

Cahuenga's One of Kind, which sells one-off movie memorabilia. At the other end of Hollywood Boulevard stands the park's centerpiece, **Mickey's Sorcerer's Hat** ①.

Behind the Sorcerer's Hat is the **Great Movie Ride**, a Magic Kingdom-style dark ride through sets from classic film scenes, from the romantic ending to *Casablanca* to scarier scenes from *Alien*. SEE ALSO SHOPPING, P.112

Sunset Boulevard

At the Sorcerer's Hat, adrenaline addicts are most likely to make a dash to the right to reach the **Rock 'n' Roller Coaster Starring Aerosmith** ② and the **Twilight Zone Tower of Terror** ③, both at the far end of Sunset Boulevard. These are the park's only thrill rides.

Other than the standard souvenir shops, the only other attraction here is **Beauty and the Beast – Live on Stage** ④, a shortened musical production of the Disney film. The nighttime spectacular **Fantasmic!** ⑤ takes place at a special stadium just behind Beauty and the Beast. SEE ALSO LIVE SHOWS, P.78; THRILL RIDES, P.125

Mickey Avenue and Animation Courtyard

Behind the Sorcerer's Hat lies Mickey Avenue and Animation Courtyard, two areas with popular behind-the-scenes attractions. **The Backlot Tour** is a half-hour tour that includes walking and riding a tram through sets used in

Left: the streets of San Francisco.

Though two vintage restaurants are located here, the **50s Prime Time Café**, a recreation of "Mom's kitchen," is the only full-service option. SEE ALSO LIVE SHOWS, P.78; RESTAURANTS, P.100

Streets of America and Commissary Lane

There's more movie magic at Streets of America. The main attraction again is a stunt show, but the **Lights, Motors, Action! Extreme Stunt Show** ⑦ only appeals to those keen on loud cars.

For the little ones the **Muppet Vision 3-D** show is a pleasant break from the heat and features Kermit and friends in a short film. The *Honey, I Shrunk the Kids* films make an appearance at their own **Movie Set Adventure**, which lets kids slide down enormous blades of grass and run away from giant insects.

If you're looking for quality Italian food head to **Mama Melrose's Ristorante Italiano**, but the park's best themed restaurant is the **Sci-Fi Dine-In Theatre Restaurant**, the only attraction of note on Commissary Lane. SEE ALSO LIVE SHOWS, P.78; RESTAURANTS, P.100–1

If you'd like to learn more about the man who started it all, **Walt Disney: One Man's Dream** on Mickey Avenue tells a sugar-coated story of Walt's life and how he began what is now one of the world's largest entertainment companies.

films and television shows. All is not always as calm as it seems, especially when you reach Catastrophe Canyon.

The Magic of Disney Animation is a much tamer affair and gives you the opportunity to see Disney animators at work. Animation Courtyard also features two live shows aimed at the little ones: the pleasant **Voyage of the Little Mermaid** and **Playhouse Disney – Live on Stage**. SEE ALSO LIVE SHOWS, P.78

Echo Lake

Stunts, stars and nostalgic dining are the attractions around Echo Lake. The **Indiana Jones Epic Stunt Spectacular** ⑥ features a Harrison Ford double recreating some of the hero archeologist's most famous stunts. **Star Tours** (minimum height: 40in) simulates a bumpy ride alongside a trainee pilot who comes into too much contact with the evil empire. **Sounds Dangerous – Starring Drew Carey** does its best to create an auditory 3-D film. Guests wear special headsets and spend a lot of time in the dark.

Below: one of the "casting" directors who entertain the crowds.

Kissimmee and Celebration

South of Walt Disney World Resort, the Irlo Bronson Memorial Highway (US 192) links the southern fringes of the park to Kissimmee and has developed into a more sprawled-out version of International Drive *(see p.24)*. Affordable accommodations dominate this long stretch of highway, with more chain restaurants and gaudy gift shops than you can count. US 192 is also the main artery for visitors staying in vacation homes. In addition to the touristy tat, there are two unique communities along this corridor: Kissimmee has a long history as the center of Florida's cattle market, while Celebration looks like a traditional small town, but is controlled solely by Disney.

Above: home-grown art.

Kissimmee and Where it all Began

It seems impossible to imagine that before Disney burst onto the scene, the sleepy town of Kissimmee was a sizeable tourist destination in its own right. People's reasons for coming were much different. Instead of families escaping for a bit of R&R, Kissimmee would get overrun by cowboys and farmers from the surrounding areas coming into town for the cattle market, rodeo, or just a bit of socializing.

Kissimmee still has a **rodeo**, and it is common to come across cattle farms alongside vacation home developments in this area, but the past is dwindling, and Kissimmee doesn't have as much to offer as it used to.

Still, the tiny streets that surround its historic center are charming for their variety of houses and people, and though the shopping will never compare with the latest malls, it does provide a flavor of small-town American life, pure and simple.

One original attraction that is still going strong is **Gator-**

> Buildings by well-known architects have made Celebration an even bigger tourist attraction. Philip Johnson, known for the New York State Theater at Lincoln Center and the Glass House of New Canaan, Connecticut, designed the town hall. Michael Graves, whose projects include Disney World's Swan and Dolphin hotels, gets credit for the post office.

land ①, one of the Orlando area's first tourist attractions. Much like its featured creature, it is proving a survivor. SEE ALSO SPORT, P.116–7; THEMED ATTRACTIONS, P.118

Between Kissimmee and Celebration

The stretch of US 192 that winds northwest from Kissimmee to Celebration is a long strip of motels, gift shops, and unique attractions that would not look out of place at a rundown funfair, if they were not so enormous.

Obviously these are built to attract idle tourists between visits to the area's larger attractions, but none of these seem to be a roaring success. One of the most disappointing is the **Old Town** ② complex. Built to resemble an

Left: Celebration is full of recreated traditional American homes.

of Celebration, but the only place to stay is the very well-appointed **Celebration Hotel**, set on the town's lake. The rest of downtown arcs around the waterfront and includes several shops and places to eat. There is a noticeable lack of chains – not what you'd expect from a corporate city. It may be no surprise that the tiny little bookshop has a section devoted to Disney, but the fact that it contains anti-Disney literature is indeed refreshing; perhaps Disney is a more relaxed puppeteer than it is usually given credit for.

One can't help feeling depressed when leaving Celebration and returning to US 192. After having spent the day in such considered environs, a land where zoning regulations are considered a limit on free speech is enough to make the most hardened patriot a bit of a socialist.

If Celebration's global planning decisions were allowed throughout Orlando, the main arteries for a tourist's stay would no longer be scars on the land, but as beautiful as either the imagined theme parks the tourists enjoy or the remarkable nature the state has always possessed.

SEE ALSO ACCOMMODATIONS, P.41

old-time main street, it does not have a worthy shop in it, though the bars and clubs like **Sun on the Beach** and funfair rides do provide plenty of distraction at night, and there is special entertainment on the weekends.

Dinner theaters play a large part in Orlando's nightlife. Some make a fantastic night out, others are less rewarding. US 192 has many to choose from, including the highly rated **Arabian Nights** ③, **Medieval Times** ④, and **Capone's Dinner and Show**. SEE ALSO LIVE SHOWS, P.80–1; NIGHTLIFE, P.94; SHOPPING, P.114

Celebration – the Town that Walt Built

Just south of the junction of Interstate 4 and US 192 is the idealized town of Celebration, a settlement designed, con-

trolled and owned by the Walt Disney Corporation. All of this makes it sound very intimidating, and it does have its limitations for residents and businesses; for visitors the overall effect is of an old-fashioned American small town. The attention to detail and well-conceived planning make a welcome relief from the brash anarchy of both US 192 and International Drive, where the only driving tenet behind construction seems to be bigger, better, louder.

There are plenty of holiday homes to be found in the town

Right: the lakeside setting for the Celebration Hotel.

Universal Studios

Universal Orlando's first theme park is now part of a complete resort capable of competing with Disney World. So, why choose Universal over Disney? Universal may not have the dreams and romance of classic Disney characters to back it up, but it isn't afraid to treat you as an adult, it revels in terrifying you, and it has bars… with happy hours. Like Hollywood Studios, Universal recreates stunts and special effects, but is happier to stick you in the middle of the action. On the downside Universal seems unable to compete with Disney in attention to detail. One trump is that Express access is available on all attractions. It is free for resort guests, for others there is a price.

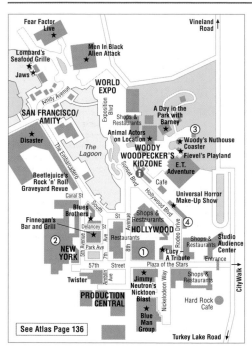

more enjoyable special-effects films in Orlando. The seats also move, but no height restrictions apply.

Across the road **Jimmy Neutron's Nicktoon Blast** (minimum height: 40in) puts you in a mini-rocket motion simulator to chase after characters from Nickelodeon, including SpongeBob Square Pants and the Rugrats.

New York

Continuing along Plaza of the Stars, Production Central becomes New York, but this big apple feels spacious and empty. Universal's biggest ride, **Revenge of the Mummy** ②, awaits, and unless you are an Express pass holder you will probably find the line anything but empty.

Less challenging for most would be a gentle exploration of **Twister**. This special-effects demonstration recreates scenes from the film of the same name to dramatic effect; some children may find this far too scary.

SEE ALSO THRILL RIDES, P.126

San Francisco/Amity

Two worlds collide in this re-creation of America's east and west coasts that features two very cheesy rides. In **Disaster** you board an under-

Production Central

Plaza of the Stars and friendly actors on set greet you as you enter the park. Beware, if you dawdle the actors may try and pull you into their scene. Straight ahead is Production Central, or you could take "Rodeo Drive" to Hollywood on the right.

Production Central has two attractions. The charm and humor of DreamWorks' Shrek films comes through in **Shrek 4-D** ①. Shrek and Princess Fiona are desperately trying to enjoy their honeymoon, but Lord Farquaad returns from the dead to ruin their plans. It is undoubtedly one of the

Left: the Blue Man Group.

of view, and **Curious George Goes to Town** ③, an interactive playground that is guaranteed to get you wet if not completely soaked. For kids ready to test their roller-coaster skills, **Woody's Nuthouse Coaster** is a gentle beginner's ride.

The **E.T. Adventure** recreates the classic film, including the bike ride past the moon, in a dark ride as good as any created by Disney.

Hollywood

Surely Tinseltown should make the biggest impact in a motion-picture theme park, but the attractions here are disappointing. The cheeky street entertainers bring the most laughs. For those with a curiosity about make-up special effects, the **Universal Horror Make-Up Show** will teach you how some of the most gruesome injuries and deformations can be accomplished.

Lucy – A Tribute pays homage to Lucille Ball, the star of the classic American sitcom *I Love Lucy*. Less lovable is the evil alien life-form that runs amok in **Terminator 2: 3-D 4**, a special-effects movie that also features live action. The show is very loud and would be frightening to small children.

---

ground train minutes before a huge earthquake strikes: it floods the tracks and threatens to dump a tanker truck on your head. While young children may find this attraction a bit scary, only young people could fall for the daftness of **Jaws**. The great white shark that disturbs this gentle cruise through Amity looks so inauthentic that the technology of Disney's Jungle Cruise *(see p. 7)* makes it look dated. The ocean theme continues at **Lombard's Seafood Grille**.

SEE ALSO RESTAURANTS, P.104

World Expo

Tucked into the corner of the park, this is a re-creation of a world's fair minus all the exhibitions. The only thing here at the time of press was **Men in Black Alien Attack** (minimum height: 42in), a ride through the universe zapping aliens along the way. Back to the Future the Ride used to

be here and was one of the finest motion simulators in Orlando. Its replacement is due in 2008.

Woody Woodpecker's Kidzone

Devoted to keeping the little ones occupied, Kidzone features two shows, the **Animal Actors on Location** and the singalong **A Day in the Park with Barney**. There are two playgrounds: **Fievel's Playland**, which presents the world from a mouse's point

Below: the vintage streets of New York.

Islands of Adventure

The screams are audible as soon as you enter the park. Look up and you'll see why – the Incredible Hulk roller coaster twists and drops riders at speeds few would think sensible. This is Orlando's finest theme park for those seeking big thrills. In total there are four roller coasters, two drenching river rides, a sensational motion simulator ride, and various fairground-style rides that throw you, spin you, drench you, and otherwise shake you all around. But it's not necessarily a kid-free zone. The comic-book-laden themes will appeal to young boys as well as overgrown ones, and the dreamlike Seuss Landing celebrates a childhood classic.

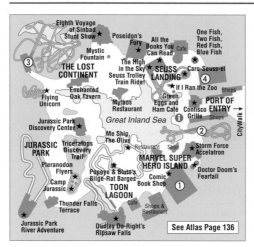

See Atlas Page 136

Port of Entry

As you enter the park you may find you need a bit of liquid courage before boarding the thrill rides. The **Confisco Grille** is a good place to steel your nerves. For most it's the area's shops that are more likely to be visited.

SEE ALSO RESTAURANTS, P.104

Marvel Super Hero Island

For boys weaned on Marvel comic books, this island is a dream come true, especially at the **Comic Book Shop;** but no cultish fascination is needed to appreciate the thrill rides here. You don't need to know

anything about Peter Parker to realize that **The Amazing Adventures of Spider Man** ① is the finest motion simulator ride in Orlando. The **Incredible Hulk Coaster** ② is the park's signature ride and not for the faint-hearted. Two standard fairground rides will please those wanting slightly tamer thrills. **Storm Force Accelatron** is a variation on the spinning teacup theme, while **Doctor Doom's Fearfall** (minimum height: 52in) lifts riders 150ft in the air before dropping them to the ground.

SEE ALSO SHOPPING, P.113; THRILL RIDES, P.126–7

Toon Lagoon

Toon Lagoon celebrates tamer cartoon characters such as Betty Boop, a spinach-craving sailor and a Canadian mountie, but the rides still pack a punch and are guaranteed to get you wet. **Dudley Do-Right's Ripsaw Falls** (minimum height: 44in) is a tame log ride for most of the journey, but its finale boasts one of the steepest water drops ever created. It is impossible to stay dry on **Popeye & Bluto's Bilge-Rat Barges** (minimum height: 42in) – if the whitewater rapids don't drench you the overhead fountains are sure to get you soaked. To make matters even worse, mischievous children can shoot water cannons at you from Popeye's **Me Ship, The Olive**.

Below: a happy fan.

Left: Marvel Super Hero Island.

SEE ALSO LIVE SHOWS, P.79; RESTAURANTS, P.105; THRILL RIDES, P.126–7

Seuss Landing

This is the most magical land outside of the Magic Kingdom. Dr Seuss's stories lend themselves to fantastic realizations, including a **Green Eggs and Ham Café**. Most remarkable is how ordinary plants and trees have been grown and pruned to resemble the zany illustrated plants in the children's book series.

Needless to say, kids are well catered for here. **If I Ran the Zoo** is an imaginative play area, and the **Caro-Seuss-el** replaces the traditional horses with Dog-alopes, Cowfish, and Aqua Mop Tops. **The High in the Sky Seuss Trolley Train Ride!** and **One Fish, Two Fish, Red Fish, Blue Fish** both lift riders above the park, with the latter promising to soak you if you can't drive your fish properly.

The Cat in the Hat ④ ride is an accomplished dark ride through the famous children's story. The couch you ride has a notorious habit of going in a spin. If you're a fan of the Cat don't leave without a trip to **All the Books You Can Read**.

SEE ALSO SHOPPING, P.113

Universal has never had the characters of Disney to capture the imagination of children. But that is about to change. In 2009, **The Wizarding World of Harry Potter** will open in Islands of Adventure. A visit to the re-creation of Hogsmeade, the mysterious Forbidden Forest, and Hogwarts castle is sure to become as coveted an experience for the magician's fans as each new book and film has been.

Jurassic Park

Dinosaurs set the theme in this jungle-like land. The **Jurassic Park Discovery Center** provides educational insight into the great beasts. You can create a dinosaur with your DNA, take control of models of these enormous animals, and if you're lucky you'll get to watch a dinosaur hatchling emerge from its shell. **Camp Jurassic** is a remarkable playground that includes a terrifying maze of caverns that little children will find frightening and big ones could lose themselves in for an entire day. Above, the **Pteranodon Flyers** whisk kids around the camp in a ski-lift-style ride.

The **Jurassic Park River Adventure** (minimum height: 42in) recreates the theme of the original film: a tourist jaunt through a park filled with dinosaurs that goes horribly wrong. Escaped raptors make trouble, but it's the T-Rex that nearly eats your boat, which is most frightening; the steep, dark drop that lets you escape him is no picnic either.

The Lost Continent

Roller coasters dominate this Atlantis-themed island. **The Flying Unicorn** is hardly tame for a kiddie coaster, but when compared to **Dueling Dragons** ③ it is definitely an easy ride.

The thrills of the roller coasters make up for the quality of the Lost Continent's other attractions. **Poseidon's Fury** is a drawn-out special-effects show set in a haunted temple. Though the live-action host is amusing, the show is not worth the wait. The **Eighth Voyage of Sindbad Stunt Show** does little to improve the standards with its stilted acting. Both attractions are saved by spectacular sets. **The Mythos** restaurant is the finest place to have a meal in the park.

International Drive and Lake Buena Vista

After the plans for Disney World were announced, Orlando Hilton owner Finley Hamilton built a hotel at the Sand Lake Road/I-4 interchange, the southern end of a road that he dubbed International Drive. The lodging seemed a long shot and became known as "Finley's Folly," but he was vindicated when Disney made the hotel its headquarters during the resort's construction, setting off a rush to develop hotels, restaurants, and competing attractions along the 12-mile commercial strip now known as I-Drive.

Above: the Peabody Orlando.

I-4 to Sand Lake Road

One of Orlando's most recognizable hotels, the **Sheraton Studio City**, towers over the northern section of International Drive, which is otherwise dominated by bargain shopping and cheap thrills. Just north of Oak Ridge Road are the **Prime Outlets**, and not much further south is the **Festival Bay Mall**, which includes the **Ron Jon Surf Shop** and the **Ron Jon Surfpark**.

Opposite Festival Bay Mall on Del Verde Way is the **Fun Spot Action Park**, with over a dozen amusement park rides, including an enormous go-cart track, but competition is fierce. **Wet'n Wild** ①, more or less across the road, is an extensive water park with slides and a wave pool, **Skyventure** is an indoor skydiving venue, while the **Magical Midway** offers more

See Atlas Pages 136, 139

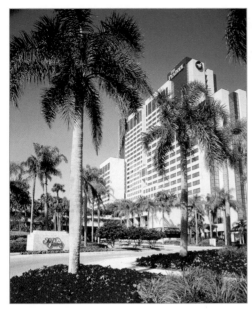

Most visitors to I-Drive and Lake Buena Vista are here for the same reason as the hoteliers and restaurateurs serving them: Disney. Even before Walt Disney officially announced the new park, developers had jumped aboard the Mouse wagon.

being redeveloped, **Pointe Orlando** is the undisputed center of International Drive's retail life. This shopping center has several bars, some of the best restaurants along the strip, and a branch of Regal Cinemas with 20 screens and including an IMAX.
SEE ALSO SHOPPING, P.114

South International Drive and Lake Buena Vista

From here International Drive continues past **SeaWorld**, but looses any inherent attraction until it terminates near the **Premium Outlets**, one of the city's largest discount malls and also home to **Dolly Parton's Dixie Stampede** ⑥, a unique experience by anyone's standards.

West of I-4 there is an assortment of hotels – some budget, some luxurious – that take advantage of the proximity to Disney World that **Lake Buena Vista** provides.
SEE ALSO SEAWORLD, P.26–7; LIVE SHOWS, P.81; SHOPPING, P.115

go-carts and fairground rides. East of International Drive on Carrier Drive is the popular **Pirate's Dinner Adventure** ②.
SEE ALSO ACCOMMODATIONS, P.44; LIVE SHOWS, P.81; SHOPPING, P.114–5; THEMED ATTRACTIONS, P.119–21, 123

South of Sand Lake Road

From Sand Lake Road to the Point, I-Drive takes on a character all its own. The I-Drive Trolley transports visitors up and down the street and, in a rare American sight, people can be seen walking along the sidewalk between restaurants and hotels that are tucked behind parking lots.

No one can call this area classy, but it is the only tourist center that combines food, drink, and hotels in such proximity that driving, much less drink-driving, is not necessary.
Ripley's Believe It or Not! ③, in a subsided building, provides oddities galore, but is not to be outdone by **Won-**

derworks ④ – a completely upside-down house full of interactive exhibits and video games. **Sleuth's Mystery Dinner Show** ⑤, in the same complex as **Goodings**, is one of the city's better dinner theaters, while expats flock to the **Best of British** pub.
SEE ALSO BARS AND CAFÉS, P.51; FOOD AND DRINK, P.69; LIVE SHOWS, P.81; THEMED ATTRACTIONS, P.118, 120

Pointe Orlando

Now that the Mercado is

Below: I–Drive has little visual appeal, but plenty of activities.

SeaWorld

With three top rides, five shows, and over a dozen restaurants, SeaWorld is much more than just the world's foremost aquarium. But the animals are the stars, and with careful planning, you can see most of them in one full day. As the emphasis is on shows and exhibits rather than rides, there tend to be fewer lines and a more easygoing pace than at other parks. Spacious grounds and the absence of themed lands encourage visitors to meander between attractions instead of marching doggedly from beginning to end. One downside is that there is no way of avoiding the long waits for Kraken and Journey to Atlantis, unless you ride during one of the main show times.

SeaWorld operates two other theme parks. The all-inclusive **Discovery Cove** gives you an up-close view of sealife and includes a chance to swim with dolphins. **Aquatica**, opening in 2008, seems like any other old water park until you realize that water slides pass underwater and through a pod of dolphins. *See Themed Attractions, p.121.*

Whale and Dolphin Theater

To the left of the entrance is a path that meanders past some modest, animal-specific attractions to the **Whale and Dolphin Theater** ①, home of the **Blue Horizons** show featuring tricky dolphins and wetsuited acrobats.

Turtle Point is a recreated lagoon that houses several endangered species of turtles. **Stingray Lagoon** is a large shallow pool filled with the creatures. Stick your hand in to feel their smooth skin. Undoubtedly the main animal attraction here is **Dolphin Cove** ②. For a couple of dollars you can buy a plate of fish at feeding time and stroke the dolphins as you feed them. There is also an underwater viewing area from which to see these playful mammals.

Plan Your Day

You'll find everything you need to organize your visit to Sea-World at the park's entrance, and as shows play such a big part here, it is worth getting a copy of the show times, sitting down with a cup of coffee at Cypress bakery and prop-

erly planning how to spend your day here – if you don't you could easily miss out on the bigger productions.

Guest Services also organizes reservations for meals and **Discovery Cove**. SEE ALSO THEMED ATTRACTIONS, P.121

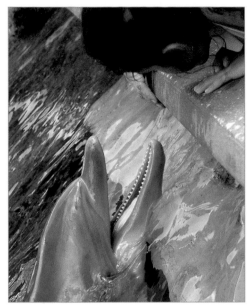

Left: friendly faces at feeding time.

is a walk-through aquarium with sharks of all descriptions. The best view is had while dining at the **Sharks Underwater Grill**. Next door is the **Nautilus Theater**, home to **Odyssea**, a mesmerizing Cirque du Soleil-style show. A short walk through the **Clydesdale Hamlet** brings you to the **Hospitality Center**, where every guest that is old enough is entitled to a free glass of beer.
SEE ALSO LIVE SHOWS, P.80; RESTAURANTS, P.109

Shamu Stadium

Opposite the SeaWorld lagoon is **Shamu Stadium** ⑦, home of the famous killer whale and his show **Believe**. **Shamu's Happy Harbor** is a disappointing play area for kids: the rides don't feel as substantial as they should, and the enormous climbing frame makes keeping an eye on your child nearly impossible.

The **Wild Arctic** hosts beluga whales and polar bears. You access the zoo section of the area via a simulated helicopter ride that goes horribly wrong.
SEE ALSO LIVE SHOWS, P.79

Things hit closer to home at **Manatee Rescue**, where the story of Florida's cuddliest-looking and most endangered sea mammal is told. An alligator pond lies just outside, displaying the state's most long-term residents.
SEE ALSO LIVE SHOWS, P.79

Thrill, Spills, and Penguins

Thrill rides and ice slides dominate the area around **Penguin Encounter** ③. The penguins themselves are fascinating to watch, and their chilled home is a perfect retreat for humans, too, during the hot summer months. The two nearby thrill rides, **Kraken** and **Journey to Atlantis**, provide danger-seeking guests with other distractions.
SEE ALSO THRILL RIDES, P.127

From Sea Lions to the Waterfront

Under the screaming shadow of Kraken sit the barking sea lions at **Pacific Point Preserve** who are more than persistent in their request for food. A trained sea lion features in **Clyde and Seamore Take Pirate Island** at the Sea Lion and Otter Stadium.

Outside lies the **Extreme Zone**, a hodge-podge of attractions including bungee cords and rock-climbing walls. Past this, the **Seaport Theater** ④ is home to the **Pets Ahoy** show.

Under the **Sky Tower** ⑤, a fixture since the park opened in 1973, the **Waterfront** area stretches along a lake at the center of the park and is the main location for sit-down restaurants such as the **Seafire Inn**.
SEE ALSO LIVE SHOWS, P.80, RESTAURANTS, P.109

Sharks, Acrobats, and Free Beer

At the top of the Waterfont are three attractions not to be missed. **Shark Encounter** ⑥

Below: an underwater surprise.

27

Downtown Orlando and Loch Haven Park

Orlando's Downtown, though the center of "real life" in central Florida, is on the fringes of Orlando's imaginary, tourist-oriented world and hence often overlooked. It shouldn't be. Around this thriving business area are quality restaurants not reliant on heavy themes to attract customers, and a thriving nightlife district meant for adults, not children. There are historic houses, grand hotels, and relaxing lakeside walks to be explored. And in Loch Haven Park, just to the north, there is another novelty: culture.

See Atlas Pages 134–135

Heading west from Downtown you will find that Division Street carries its name for a reason. To its east lies commerce-driven Downtown Orlando, to the west the city's traditional African-American neighborhood, which dates back to the early 1900s. The **Wells Built Museum** documents the area's vibrant past. *See also Museums and Galleries, p.84*

many businesses struggling to survive on their own.

From Church Street to Washington Street, there is a medley of bars that would seem more appropriate on a college campus than in a business center.

But there is culture here, too. At 29 Orange Avenue is the **Cityartsfactory**, now housed in the old Philips Theater. This is the center for the Downtown Arts District and features a large exhibition space and several commercial art galleries.

North of Central Boulevard is **Wall Street Plaza**, a bar and restaurant complex with happy-hour specials to tempt in the office workers. Most nights feature live music in one of the bars. Walk through Wall Street Plaza to Heritage Square and the **Orange**

Downtown

Orange Avenue from South Street to East Colonial Drive is the spine of Downtown Orlando. At its southern base is the **Westin Grand Bohemian** ①, a top-class hotel that includes the **Boheme**, one of the city's finest restaurants, and the **Grand Bohemian Gallery**,

which features a fine collection of European and American art.

Just west of here, between I-4 and Orange Avenue, is the revitalized **Church Street Station** ② area. This complex has had its fair share of problems. Once the center of Downtown's nightlife, redevelopment has taken much longer than expected, leaving

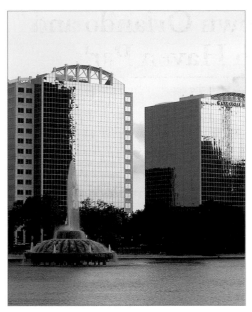

Left: Downtown's Lake Eola.

complex, hosting the Philharmonic orchestra, theater productions, and the **Orlando Magic** basketball team.
SEE ALSO, MUSIC, DANCE, AND THEATRE, P.88; SPORT, P.116

Loch Haven Park

Loch Haven was created as a cultural anchor, a counterbalance to the theme parks' domination, and includes heavy hitters such as the **Orlando Science Center** ⑤ and **Orlando Museum of Art** ⑥. But culture shouldn't have to be treated like this.

Though originally meant as a cultural oasis, it feels more like a ghetto. While intriguing institutions such as **The Rep Theatre**, the **Orlando Shakespeare Theater** ⑦ and the **Menello Museum of American Art** are located here, there is nothing tempting you to stay beyond your visit – the nearest restaurants, bars, and cafés are Downtown – a 10-minute drive away. Each attraction has its own isolated parking lot, hardly an invitation to walk between institutions.

Just to the east of Loch Haven Park are the extensive **Harry P. Leu Gardens**, which include wide-ranging examples of Florida's natural flora.
SEE ALSO MUSEUMS AND GALLERIES, P.84–5, 87; MUSIC, DANCE, AND THEATER, P.89; NATURAL WORLD, P.91

County Regional History Center. This old courthouse now tells the story of central Florida's development.

Magnolia Avenue ③ is worth exploring as well; in some ways it's an artier Orange Avenue. It has several galleries, the **Mad Cow Theatre** and more sophisticated drinking spots like the **Harp & Celt**.
SEE ALSO ACCOMMODATIONS, P.47–8; BARS AND CAFÉS, P.52–3; MUSEUMS AND GALLERIES, P.83, 85, 86; MUSIC, DANCE, AND THEATER, P.89; RESTAURANTS, P.109–10

Lake Eola and Thornton Park

To the east of Downtown between Central and Robinson streets, the 43-acre Lake Eola Park has a gentle walking trail and a café with fine views of the lake. Paddleboats can be rented if you'd like to venture out to the central fountain, and a small amphitheater hosts concerts.

Overlooking the lake is the **Eö Inn**, a historic boutique hotel with the full-service **Urban Spa**. South of the lake is the Thornton Park area, where you'll find trendy places to eat and drink such as **The Beacon.**
SEE ALSO ACCOMMODATIONS, P.47; PAMPERING, P.97; RESTAURANTS, P.109

Centroplex

Home to the **Bob Carr Performing Arts** ④ venue and **Amway Arena**, this is Orlando's main entertainment

Below: a vintage train at the refurbished Church Street Station.

Winter Park and Maitland

North of Orlando lies an oasis of small-town American life with a healthy helping of sophisticated European atmosphere – Winter Park. This town thrives on the energy of Rollins College, an elite liberal arts institute that runs several museums open to students and tourists alike. Park Avenue is the center of day- and nightlife in Winter Park, with numerous independently owned shops and some fantastic cafés for lunch, and fine dining options for dinner. Beyond Winter Park to the northeast is Maitland, whose historical society commemorates all aspects of its history, and Eatonville, the first African-American township in the United States.

Below: the romantic setting of Rollins College.

Park Avenue

If you find yourself in Orlando for reasons not entirely of your own choosing – kids' vacation, a convention, visiting in-laws in holiday homes – then Park Avenue could prove the perfect antidote to the theme-park atmosphere.

This tiny main street of Winter Park is lined with places for adults to enjoy such pleasures as a quiet glass of red at the **Wine Room**, a fine meal at **Café de France** and other treats more sophisticated than Mickey Mouse ice creams; and there is not a themed restaurant in sight.

At the northern end of Park Avenue's string of shops and restaurants is the **Charles Hosmer Morse Museum of American Art** ①, which celebrates the leaded-glass works of Louis Comfort Tiffany.

SEE ALSO FOOD AND DRINK, P.69; MUSEUMS AND GALLERIES, P.85; RESTAURANTS, P.111

Rollins College ②

The graceful Spanish-style architecture that constitutes the campus of **Rollins College** creates a tranquil, leafy retreat on the shores of Lake Virginia, east of Park Avenue and south of Holt Avenue.

In addition to providing a terrific setting for an afternoon

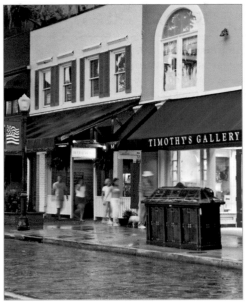

Left: small shops dominate Park Avenue.

It does not take an avid "twitcher" to spot the numerous birds of prey circling Florida's skies and even rummaging through the garbage bins on I-Drive. If these feathered friends have intrigued you, then this is the perfect place to find out more as injured birds are nursed back to health on the premises.

Eatonville today is a nice, quiet small town that you could easily drive straight through, but it has great significance in US history. After the Emancipation Proclamation freed the slaves in 1863, Eatonville became one of the first all-black towns in America. In 1887 it officially became the first incorporated African-American town in the United States. Unless you visit during the annual festival, this history is hard to spot. Only the **Zora Neale Hurston National Museum of Arts** ⑥ stands out. Named after the Harlem Renaissance writer who grew up here, it now celebrates African-American art.

SEE ALSO MUSEUMS AND GALLERIES, P.82, 83, 86, 87; NATURAL WORLD, P.90

---

stroll, the college maintains some fine museums, on and off campus, in the Orlando area. The small but refined **Cornell Fine Arts Museum** ③ features strong temporary exhibitions and a modest collection of European art. Also on campus is the eclectic **Annie Russell Theatre**.
SEE ALSO MUSEUMS AND GALLERIES, P.85; MUSIC, DANCE, AND THEATER, P.89

Greater Winter Park

Rollins College's cultural institutions extend beyond the campus grounds. To the northeast along Osceola Avenue are the **Albin Polasek Museum and Sculpture Gardens** ④, which exhibit the Czech sculptor's work. Attractions become more Floridian at the **Winter Park Village** shopping center, which includes several restaurants and bars.
SEE ALSO MUSEUMS AND GALLERIES, P.85; SHOPPING, P.115

Maitland and Eatonville

Sleepy Maitland has tried its best to tag along to Winter Park's "real world" ability to attract tourists, but lacking a genuine main street, it doesn't receive the same attention. Instead it has the Maitland Historical Society, which runs two intriguing museums. The **Waterhouse Residence Museum and Carpentry Shop Museum** on the shores of Lake Lily preserve what life was like in central Florida at the beginning of the 20th century, while the **Maitland Historical Museum and Telephone Museum** keep an eclectic collection based on local lore. Next door to the Telephone Museum, the **Maitland Art Center** runs courses and has a small gallery set amid its remarkable Aztec-inspired grounds.

Between Maitland and Eatonville lies the **Audubon Center for Birds of Prey** ⑤.

Below: the Aztec-inspired Maitland Art Center.

The Space Coast

There is more than enough to do in Orlando, but the Space Coast offers a once-in-a-lifetime opportunity. Nowhere else in the world are you able to visit up close a location that launches satellites and humans into space. The visitor center is full of compelling exhibitions, from how man first reached the Moon to the latest developments in the International Space Station. The security necessary for these operations has preserved Florida's natural habitats all along this stretch of coast – don't be surprised to spot an alligator outside your tour bus – and nearby towns such as Cocoa Beach provide fine surfing and more earthly distractions.

Above: a rare chance to meet an astronaut.

Kennedy Space Center ①

Though you may initially think the Space Center's Visitor Complex is small, it takes an entire day to see it, as the bus tour itself takes 2–3 hours.

Educational exhibits are to the left as you exit the Information Center. **Nature and Technology** covers the unique natural environment surrounding the Space Center. **Early Space Exploration** tells of the traumas and triumphs that led to the first landing on the Moon, while in the mesmerising **Rocket Garden** genuine examples from these early days tower above visitors. The **Children's Play Dome** will entertain any of those young ones not interested in space – it's usually rather empty.

Opposite the Information Center is the **Mad Mission to Mars: 2025**, a 3-D and special-effects film through about traveling space. Beyond that is the **IMAX** theater building which shows two features: *Space Station 3D* and *Walking on the Moon 3D*.

To the right of the Information Center is a quirky exhibit called **Robot Scouts**, which celebrates these often forgotten, mechanical space heroes. Beyond that is a life-size shuttle that you can explore independently, and the **Shuttle Launch Experience**, which lets you know just what it feels like to be on a shuttle

Left: the Rocket Garden.

disappointment after this, even though you get to observe technicians preparing segments of the Space Station for launch.
SEE ALSO THRILL RIDES, P.127

Merritt Island and Canaveral Seashore

In contrast to all this high-tech adventure are two nearby nature preserves: the **Merritt Island National Wildlife Refuge** ②, home to manatees and leatherback turtles alike, and the barrier dunes and sea-swept beaches of **Canaveral National Seashore** ③.
SEE ALSO NATURAL WORLD, P.90–1

Cocoa Beach ④

Those who prefer beaches in a more developed setting will find Cocoa Beach to their liking – an old-time seaside town with an abundance of chain motels, restaurants, and souvenir shops, as well as first-rate beaches. The biggest attraction is the **Ron Jon Surf Shop**, a neon-lit palace devoted to surf gear. Famous surfers occasionally drop in for autograph sessions; scuba diving and surfing lessons are also available.
SEE ALSO SHOPPING, P.115

mission. This lacks the centrifugal force of Mission: SPACE at Epcot *(see p.124)*, so don't be put off by it.

At the back of the Visitor Center there is a **Launch Status Center** that briefs visitors about upcoming missions of all kinds, and an **Astronaut Memorial** for those who have given their life in the cause of space exploration.

The bus tour from the visitor complex takes in three sights. The first is the **LC-39 Observation Gantry**, which has a short film about the early space program, but the key objective is to gain good views of the dozen or so launch pads from the gantry above. Many of these launch pads are

still active. You'll pass the Space Shuttle's enormous **Vehicle Assembly Building** on your way to and from here.

The **Apollo/Saturn V Center** could be a visitor center on its own, with its 363ft-long Apollo rocket and a re-creation of an Apollo launch and the first Moon landing.

The International **Space Station Center** is a bit of a

For those looking to continue their journey into space, the **U.S. Astronaut Hall of Fame** is just across the Indian River from the Visitor Center along SR 405. *See Themed Attractions, p.119.*

Below: Cocoa Beach Pier as the sun goes down.

A–Z

In the following section Orlando's attractions and services are organized by theme, under alphabetical headings. Items that link to another theme are cross-referenced. All sights that fall within the bounds of the atlas section at the end of the book are given a page number and grid reference.

Accommodations

Accommodations in Orlando range from luxury resorts that cater to your every whim to modest mom-and-pop motels, antique-filled bed & breakfasts, and campgrounds. Although standards for service and facilities are generally quite high, there is the occasional bad apple. Indeed, some of the cheapest accommodations offered by tour operators are positively miserable, so be sure you know what you're getting into before signing on the dotted line. If you're staying at Disney spend the extra money to stay at a resort they classify as Moderate or Deluxe – the attention to detail at these resorts guarantee a magical vacation.

Left: the monorail travels through the Contemporary's main lobby.

which for many hotels is a lean time.

Florida also imposes a resort tax, in addition to the usual sales tax, which is added to the price of all hotel rooms. It varies from county to county and ranges from between 2 and 5 percent.

Reservations and Prices

Reservations are generally required, and if you are traveling during the high season you should book several months ahead if you have your heart set on a particular hotel or if you want to stay inside Walt Disney World.

Room rates vary enormously between the high season and the low season (see box p.42). There is plenty of scope to ask for a discount if you are staying for a week or more, or if you are visiting during the off-season,

Magic Kingdom Resorts

Contemporary Resort

4600 North World Drive, Lake Buena Vista; tel: 407-824-1000; $$$; Monorail to Epcot and Magic Kingdom, Link: 302; map p.138 B4

The monorail passes through the middle of this 15-story A-frame built over a quarter-century ago. Most rooms have two queen-size beds and a daybed. Tower rooms have private balconies overlooking the Magic Kingdom or Bay Lake; those in the Garden Wings have nice views but are somewhat distant from the central property. There are several bars and restaur-

Information on all of Disney's resort hotels can be found at www.disneyworld.com. Reservations can be made there or by phoning tel: 407-939-6244.

ants, including the elegant **California Grill** – a popular spot for watching Magic Kingdom fireworks. Amenities include a supervised evening children's program, salon, water activities, a health club and tennis center, several swimming pools, and a video arcade.
SEE ALSO RESTAURANTS, P.102

Grand Floridian Resort & Spa

4401 Grand Floridian Way, Lake Buena Vista; tel: 407-824-3000; $$$; monorail to Epcot and Magic Kingdom, boat to Magic Kingdom; map p.138 A4

The Victorian era in all its splendor is recreated at Disney's flagship property, an elegant confection of glistening white, wooden buildings with red shingled roofs, gracious verandas, and turrets. Open-cage elevators in the plant-filled, five-story, chandeliered lobby serve

Left: the grand lobby of the Wilderness Lodge has several nooks with open fireplaces and sofas to relax in.

All of Disney's resorts are connected to all of Disney's parks by bus. Some resorts are connected to individual parks by monorail or boat – a great way to arrive. We have listed these unique links in our listings.

second-floor shops and restaurants. Most rooms in the four- and five-story lodge buildings have two queen-size beds and a daybed; many overlook the Seven Seas Lagoon. Amenities include some of Disney's finest dining experiences at **Victoria and Albert's** and **Citricos**, and a fine waterside restaurant, **Narcoossee's**; several bars, a supervised evening children's program, the Grand Floridian Health Club and Spa, several swimming pools, and water activities.
SEE ALSO PAMPERING, P.96;
RESTAURANTS, P.102–3

Polynesian Resort
1600 Seven Seas Drive, Lake Buena Vista; tel: 407-824-2000; $$$; Monorail to Magic Kingdom and Epcot, boat to Magic Kingdom, Link: 302; map p.138 A4
One of Disney's most authentic theme hotels re-

creates a Pacific Islands retreat. The centerpiece is the Great Ceremonial House, a tropical extravaganza of plants and waterfalls. Rooms, in 11 two- and three-story "longhouses," vary in size, but most have two queen-size beds, a daybed, and balconies. Those overlooking the Seven Seas Lagoon afford front-row seats for Magic Kingdom fireworks. There

are several restaurants and bars, two pools, a playground, supervised evening children's programs, and water activities.

Wilderness Lodge and Villas
901 Timberline Drive, Lake Buena Vista; tel: 407-824 3200; $$$; boat to Magic Kingdom, Link: 302; map p.138 B4
A skillful blending of wood and stone replicates the look of an early 20th-century National Park lodge. Although the eight-story lakefront dwelling appears rustic, accommodations are anything but. Most rooms have two queen-size beds, tables and chairs, and

Below: the Grand Floridian Resort and Spa.

Prices for a standard double room:
$ under $100
$$ $100–$200
$$$ over $200

balconies. Villas, in a five-story adjoining building, range from studios with kitchenettes to two-bedroom units with dining areas, kitchens, and whirlpool tubs. There are several restaurants and bars, a supervised evening children's program, a health club, video arcade, swimming pool, sand beach, and boat rental. Boats sail to the Magic Kingdom; buses serve the other parks.

Epcot Resorts

Boardwalk Resort and Villas
2101 Epcot Resorts Boulevard, Lake Buena Vista; tel: 407-939-5100; $$$; boat to Epcot; map p.138 B2

Elaborately detailed buildings with turreted, brightly colored facades and twinkling lights recreate an East Coast boardwalk circa 1920. Spacious rooms with ocean-blue and sea-green furnishings have two queen-size brass beds, daybeds, and ceiling fans; two-story garden suites have private gardens. The villas – Disney Vacation Club timeshare units – sleep 4 to 12 and have kitchens, laundries, whirlpool tubs, and VCRs. Nightclubs, restaurants, midway games, and shops line the boardwalk. There's a supervised evening

children's program, a health club, and a large swimming pool with a 200-ft water slide.

Caribbean Beach
900 Cayman Way, Lake Buena Vista; tel: 407-934-3400; $$; Link 301; map p.138 C2

Each of the five areas at this brightly colored resort that circles 45-acre Barefoot Bay recreates a Caribbean island and has its own pool, beach, and laundry room. Accommodations in each of the two-story buildings are the same: two double beds, a table and chairs, a coffeemaker, and bath. Rates vary only according to view. A food court and several casual restaurants cater to the resort's family-oriented clientele, and there are water sports, bike rentals, playgrounds, a shopping complex, and a video arcade.

Dolphin Hotel
1200 Epcot Resorts Boulevard, Lake Buena Vista; tel: 407-934-4000; $$$; boat to Epcot; map p.138 B2

Two 56-ft-high dolphins and hundreds of seven-story banana leaves festoon the facade of this 27-story, triangular, turquoise hotel with four nine-story wings. The lobby has a circus theme, and the spacious rooms, with turquoise and peach furnishings, have two queen-size beds, desks,

and chairs. Some have balconies. There is a supervised evening children's program. In addition to the seashell-shaped pool there are several restaurants and lounges on the property, which is within walking distance of Epcot and the BoardWalk.

Old Key West Resort
1510 North Cove Road, Lake Buena Vista; tel: 407-827-7700; $$$; boat to Downtown Disney; map p.138 C2

Although it's miles from the ocean, this hotel's color scheme and architecture bear an uncanny resemblance to buildings in the seaside resort town far to the south. Studios have two queen-size beds, tables and chairs, small refrigerators, microwaves, and coffeemakers. One-bedroom villas have king-size beds in the main bedroom and queen-size sleeper sofas in the living room. Two- and three-bedroom villas have full kitchens and porches or balconies. All units except studios have private whirlpool tubs. There are grills and picnic tables, several restaurants, a health club, swimming pools, shopping, tennis courts, a video arcade, and playgrounds.

Port Orleans – French Quarter
2201 Orleans Drive, Lake Buena Vista; tel: 407-934-5000; $$; boat to Downtown Disney; map p.138 C3

Left: the Boardwalk Villas are part of Disney's timeshare scheme.

This moderate hotel is reminiscent of New Orleans, and its landscaping makes it very suitable for couples wanting to get away as there are many quiet, romantic spots in which to linger. On the other hand, kids will love the Doubloon Lagoon pool with its colorfully themed attractions that include alligator and dragon slides.

Port Orleans – Riverside
1251 Riverside Drive, Lake Buena Vista; tel: 407-934-6000; $$; boat to Downtown Disney; map p.138 C3

The former Dixie Landings has been renamed but retains the feel of the Old South. Accommodations are in two- and three-story buildings divided into "parishes." All rooms are the same size, and most have two double beds. Mansion rooms are in antebellum-style "estates," while Bayou rooms are in rustic-appearing buildings surrounding Man Island, a sprawling water complex. Only mansions have elevators. Amenities include six swimming pools, a restaurant and food court, shops, bars, bike and boat rentals, and fishing excursions.

Fort Wilderness Resort within Walt Disney World has more than 800 campsites for tents and RVs. Another option is to rent a trailer (decked out like a log cabin) that sleeps up to six people and has air conditioning, color TV, radio, cookware, and linen, i.e. all the equipment you'll need. The resort is located amid 650 acres of woods and streams on Bay Lake, east of the Magic Kingdom. For information and reservations, tel: 407-824-2900.

Above: the Swan Hotel is one of Disney's finest resorts and is especially suitable for people traveling without children.

Swan Hotel
1200 Epcot Resorts Boulevard; tel: 407-934-3000; $$$; boat to Epcot; map p.138 B2

Just across the road from the Dolphin is this Westin property, topped by two 47ft-tall swans. Rooms in the 12-story main building and two seven-story towers are a bit smaller in size than those in the Dolphin (see p.38), but similar in color and amenities. There's a pool as well as several restaurants and bars, including the fine **Il Mulino's** and **Kimono** sushi bar, and a supervised evening children's program.

SEE ALSO RESTAURANTS, P.103

Yacht and Beach Club and Beach Club Villas
1800 Epcot Boulevard, Lake Buena Vista; tel: 407-934-7000 (Yacht Club) and 407-934-8000 (Beach Club); $$$; boat to Epcot, Link: 303; map p.138 B2

Each of the three properties overlooking a 25-acre lake has a distinct theme, but they share many facilities. Yacht Club rooms are finished in a nautical motif; those in the Beach Club are reminiscent of a private seaside retreat. Most, however, have either one king-size or two queen-size beds (some with

daybeds), ceiling fans, and a table with chairs. The studios and one- to three-bedroom villas sleep up to eight. The resort's highlight is Storm-along Bay, an elaborate swimming area with whirlpools, water slides, and a private beach. In addition, there are several pools, a miniature golf course, a health club, restaurants and bars, boating, a supervised evening children's program, a salon, tennis courts, a video arcade, and shops.

Animal Kingdom Resorts
All-Star Movies, Music, and Sports
1991 West Buena Vista Drive, Lake Buena Vista; tel: 407-939 7000 (All-Star Movies), 407-939 6000 (All-Star Music), 407-939 5000 (All-Star Sports); $$; Link: 303, 305; map p.138 A1–B1

This was Disney's only budget complex until the Pop Century (see p.40) opened. It has 30 three-story buildings divided by themes. Each has a distinctive facade, but aside from a few decorative touches, the size and decor of most rooms are identical: they're 260sq ft, have two double beds, small bureaus, a table with chairs, and bathrooms with sepa-

39

Above: the wildlife comes to see you at the Animal Kingdom Lodge.

rate vanity areas. Popular with families, the resort has a game room, playground, outdoor pool, shopping, and food court. Buses transport guests to the parks.

Animal Kingdom Lodge
2901 Osceola Parkway, Lake Buena Vista; tel: 407-938-3000; Link: 301; map p.138 A1

Built to resemble a southern African game lodge, the hotel has an elaborately furnished lobby with a four-story observation window looking out onto a 33-acre savanna, which teems with wildlife. All standard and deluxe rooms have hand-crafted furniture and traditional tapestries, and balconies; most have two queen-size beds. Many of the balconies overlook the savanna. Amenities include three restaurants, several bars, a children's play area that opens at 4.30pm, a health club, playground, shopping area, video arcade, and outdoor pool.

Right: Downtown Disney as seen from the Hilton.

Disney–MGM Resorts

Coronado Springs Resort
1000 West Buena Vista Drive, Lake Buena Vista; tel: 407-939-1000; $$$; Link: 303, 305; map p.138 B2

The American Southwest and Mexico are elaborately re-created at this lakefront complex with outdoor fountains, a Mayan pyramid, and the country's largest ballroom (the property is a popular spot for conventions). Each of three buildings is evocative of a different setting – the oceanfront, the city, and the countryside – with rooms decorated accordingly. Standard rooms have two double

beds: some queens and kings are also available. There are several pools, a large whirlpool, a health club and spa, a playground, video arcades, shops, a restaurant and food court, several bars, and water sports.

Pop Century
901 Century Drive, Lake Buena Vista; tel: 407-938-4000; $$; Link 301; map p.138 C1

Encompassing 20 four-story buildings, this resort is divided into two sections: the Legendary Years, depicting the first 50 years of the 20th century, and the Classic Years, depicting the second 50 years. Statues representing various aspects of pop culture are used to carry the themes. Rooms, smaller than at other Disney properties at 260sq ft, have two double beds, bathrooms with a separate vanity area, and small dressers, tables, and chairs. Each section has a food court, swimming pool, playground, shopping area, and video arcade.

Other Disney Resorts

Buena Vista Palace
1900 Buena Vista Drive, Lake Buena Vista; tel: 866-397-6516; www.buenavistapalace.com; $$; map p.139 D2

Located across the lagoon from Downtown Disney, the Palace's rooms are all very well appointed in sleek modern furnishings and pillow-top beds. Most have outdoor balconies, and some even offer a view of the lake. The Island Suites provide more space than the smallish rooms. The resort has large spa and pool facilities and six restaurants to choose from.

Above: the stylishly southern Celebration Hotel.

Grosvenor Resort

1850 Hotel Plaza Boulevard, Lake Buena Vista; tel: 407-828 4444; www.grosvenorresort.com; $$$; map p.139 D2

One of several hotels on Disney property but not actually operated by the Disney Company, the Grosvenor is a middle-of-the-road lakeside resort with convention facilities and comfortable, if not lavish, rooms. A variety of recreational facilities and restaurants is available. There is also the **Murderwatch Mystery Theater** dinner show on Saturday night. Free transportation to the parks is provided for all guests.

SEE ALSO LIVE SHOWS, P.81

Hilton

1751 Hotel Plaza Boulevard, Lake Buena Vista; tel: 407-827-

4000; www.hilton-wdwv.com; $$$; map p.139 D2

Within walking distance to Downtown Disney, this large hotel is set among 23 acres of tropical landscaping. Hotel guests receive similar benefits as Disney Resort guests, including Extra Magic Hours, an on-site Disney Character breakfast, free transportation to the parks, and access to five Disney golf courses. Several grades of suite are available for those needing more space. All rooms have Hilton Serenity Beds to provide extra comfort and an MP3 compatible clock radio.

Royal Plaza Hotel

1905 Hotel Plaza Boulevard, Lake Buena Vista; tel: 407-828-2828; www.royalplaza.com; $$; map p.139 D2

Located near Downtown Disney, the Royal Plaza was refurbished in 2007. Its standard rooms are the largest in the Downtown Disney area, are appointed with subtle contemporary decor and furnishings, and have all the modern amenities you'd expect. Suites are also available. The pool is nothing to shout about, but being this close to Disney, you may not find time to use it.

Celebration and Kissimmee

Celebration Hotel

700 Bloom Street, Celebration; tel: 407-566-6000 or 888-499-3800; www.celebration hotel.com; $$$; map p.18

Located in the town of Celebration, this quietly elegant, out-of-the-way boutique hotel seems like a million miles away from Disney World, which is just next door. Guests feel like they are stepping back into Old Florida. Registration is concierge-style in the low-key lobby, which features comfy sofas, fans, a bar, and hand-painted murals and hand-tinted photos of orange groves, wildlife, and historic scenes. The peaceful terrace has rocking chairs and overlooks the pool, lake, and adjoining workout room. The 115 rooms have a classic southern feel, with pinstriped wallpaper, reproduction antique furnishings, CD players, interactive televisions, and high-speed internet and e-mail access; some have balconies. Guests may play Celebration's renowned 18-hole golf course and work out at the state-of-the-art fitness

41

Orlando hotel prices vary quite dramatically between the seasons, which are unsurprisingly linked to the US school calendar. The Christmas break period, mid–Dec until New Year, is the most expensive, followed by spring break, mid-Feb until the end of Mar, and summer, end of May until the beginning of August. The cheapest times to visit are from New Year until mid-Feb, Aug and Sept (but be prepared for extraordinary heat), and the first half of Dec.

Above: arriving in style at Portofino Bay.

center at Celebration's nearby hospital.

Celebrity Resorts
2800 North Pionciana Boulevard, Kissimmee; tel: 866-507-1429; www.celebrity resorts.com; $$

This timeshare establishment has several different sizes of accommodation, from standard rooms to three-bedroom villas. All are quite affordable and available for short lets. The resort has tennis, basketball and racquetball courts, a fitness center, three outdoor pools and one indoor pool, and a playground. The rooms and suites are well designed, making the most of their space.

Mystic Dunes Resort and Golf Club
7900 Mystic Dunes Lane, Celebration; tel: 407-226-9501 or 877-747-4747; www.mystic-dunes-resort. com; $$$

Located on 600 acres of meticulously landscaped grounds, this timeshare resort makes for a grand short-term retreat. The sleekly furnished, one- to three-bed villas all have a fully equipped kitchen, washer and dryer, and a whirlpool bath. Resort amen-

ities include the **Mystic Dunes Golf Club**, four heated swimming pools (one of which has a two-story water slide and children's wading pool), mini-golf, tennis, and basketball courts.
SEE ALSO GOLF, P.71

Omni Orlando Resort at ChampionsGate
1500 Masters Boulevard, ChampionsGate; tel: 407-390-6664; www.omniorlando resort.com; $$$

Located southwest of Celebration along the I-4 corridor, this luxury resort is surrounded by 36 holes of golf, all designed by Greg Norman. It is also home to the **David Leadbetter Golf Academy**. No prizes for guessing what brings most guests here. For those not wanting to golf, there is a big pool with water slide, a lazy river, and seven restaurants to keep you busy.
SEE ALSO GOLF, P.70

Prices for a standard double room:
$ under $100
$$ $100–$200
$$$ over $200

Orange Lake Resort and Country Club
8505 West Irlo Bronson Memorial Highway (US 192), Kissimmee; tel: 407-239-0000 or 800-877-6522; www.orange lake.com; $$$

This handsomely constructed lakeside resort complex has several pools set in beautiful landscaped grounds. The two- and three-bedroom suites feel spacious and inviting and have all the amenities you'd require on holiday, even a kitchenette. There is also a small lazy river to float down, and the Splash lagoon pool has a water slide to entertain children. For bigger boys and girls there are four championship golf courses to choose from.
SEE ALSO GOLF, P.72

Palm Lakefront Hostel
4840 West Irlo Bronson Highway (US 192), Kissimmee; tel: 407-396-1759; www.orlando hostels.com; $; Link: 54, 55

The only place in Orlando that properly caters to the backpacking crowd: you can get a bed for less than twenty bucks at times, and a public bus connects it directly to Disney and other theme parks. Of course this isn't luxury accommodation, but it sure ain't bad. With a clean pool and a lakeside view, it is more than serviceable.

Seralago Suites Maingate East

5678 West Irlo Bronson Memorial Highway (US 192), Kissimmee; tel: 407-396-4488 or 800-366-5437; www.seralago suites.com; $; map p.139 D1

The concept behind this large, family-oriented hotel near the Magic Kingdom is a winner: kidsuites and two-room suites that cost less than $100 dollars a night – ideal if you are on a budget and insist on putting little ones to bed in a different space. The quality of the hotel, though, is no better than you'd expect for these prices. The rooms are as dull and dreary as any Motel 6 chain, the kidsuites are only one room with a fort built around the children's bunk beds, and even the 2-room suites feel a bit cramped (though they are still the best bargain in the area). The pool not only lacks any unique

Above: the Royal Pacific Resort.

design, but is also missing the most essential quality for most families: shade. There is a shuttle service to the park once a day.

Universal Studios Resorts

Hard Rock Hotel

5800 Universal Boulevard, Orlando; tel: 407-503-2000; $$$; map p.136 A3

Not quite as lavish or expensive as the Portofino, the accommodations at this Mission-style hotel range from very comfortable standard rooms to large and opulent suites. An eclectic array of rock-and-roll memorabilia is displayed tastefully around the building, which nearly surrounds a huge

pool with a sandy beach, water slide, and underwater sound system. Several restaurants and bars, a fitness room, an indoor play area, and a Hard Rock store round out the picture.

Portofino Bay Hotel

5601 Universal Boulevard, Orlando; tel: 407-503-1000; $$$; map p.136 A3

This is such a beautifully designed and constructed re-creation of the real Portofino, you'd be forgiven for calling out *buon giorno* from your window first thing in the morning, especially after that first cup of stiff Italian coffee. Set on a harbor filled with fishing boats, the hotel offers some of the most luxurious accommodations in Orlando, with large, sumptuous rooms, three elaborate pools, a spa, an indoor children's play area, and several restaurants, including the elegant Delfino Riviera. Very expensive, but worth it. Free water taxis transport guests between the theme parks and the three Universal hotels. Best of all, guests at all on-site hotels are given Express access to nearly all rides and attractions.

Royal Pacific Resort

6300 Hollywood Way, Orlando;

Below: all the mod cons, and a guitar at the Hard Rock Hotel.

43

Don't forget to check the hidden charges when booking a hotel. All hotels add a Bed Tax, which varies from county to county and can be as high as 5 percent. Also, do not make any in-room calls until you check the rates (these should be provided near the phone). Local and toll-free calls are usually free, but not always; and when they are not, they usually cost much, much more than they should.

Above: the candlelit pool at Gaylord Palms – a romantic place for a rendezvous.

tel: 407-503-3000; $$$; map p.136 A3

Attempting to recreate the South Pacific in central Florida, this resort – opened in 2002 – is centered around a lagoon-like pool fringed with palm trees, waterfalls, a sandy beach, and cabanas. Accommodations are priced slightly lower than the Hard Rock Hotel but sacrifice little in the way of comfort or amenities, which include six restaurants and bars, a children's activity room, a fitness room, and convention facilities.

International Drive and Lake Buena Vista

Arnold Palmer's Bay Hill Club & Lodge
9000 Bay Hill Boulevard, Orlando; tel: 888-422-9445; www.bayhill.com; $$$

Duffers are in heaven at this golf resort, where they can play two championship courses or brush up their techniques in the **Arnold Palmer Golf Academy**. The atmosphere at the wood-and-stone lodge is low-key and clubby, with nicely appointed rooms. Arnie is often in residence during the winter months.
SEE ALSO GOLF, P.70

Caribe Royale
8101 World Center Drive, Orlando; tel: 800-823-8300; www.cariberoyale.com; $$; Link 304; map p.139 D2

This enormous resort has over 1,200 suites and over 100 villas. Each suite has either two queen beds or one king, a wet bar, microwave, refrigerator, and coffeemaker. Each suite has a full kitchen, washer and dryer. The main pool has a 75-ft water slide. Other amenities include tennis courts, a video arcade, fitness centre, basketball court, and free transportation to Disney World. Their flagship restaurant, **The Venetian Room,** offers fine Italian cuisine.
SEE ALSO RESTAURANTS, P.109

Below: inside the Gaylord Palms Resort.

Castle DoubleTree Resort
8629 International Drive, Orlando; tel: 407-345-1511; www.doubletreecastle.com; $$; I-Ride: mainline; map p.136 A1

Spires, mosaics, banners, and rich purple-and-gold drapes and bedspreads give this mid-range hotel a touch of medieval whimsy. Amenities include two restaurants, a fitness center, free shuttles to the theme parks, and a pleasant courtyard pool.

Enclave Suites at Orlando
6165 Carrier Drive, Orlando; tel: 407-351-1155 or 800-457-0077; www.enclavesuites.com; $$; I-Ride: mainline; map p.136 A2

Located just off of International Drive, this all-suites hotel offers a lot more than the average chain. All rooms include a fully-fitted kitchen, and the Kid Suites are decorated in theme-park style. There are two outdoor pools and one indoor pool, two kiddie pools, and a playground to keep everyone busy.

Four Points by Sheraton Orlando Studio City
5905 International Drive, Orlando; tel: 407-351-2100; www.sheraton.com/studiocity; $$; I-Ride: main and green lines, Link: 8, 38; map p.136 A2

The design of Studio City is much more than you'd expect for a mid-priced

Above: ice slide at the Gaylord Palms Resort.

hotel. The rooms are a bit too trendy, with zebra-striped shower curtains and other "trying too hard" touches, but the views in the upper rooms make up for this shortcoming, and all the rooms, up high or down low, are generously sized.

Gaylord Palms Resort & Convention Center
6000 West Osceola Parkway, Kissimmee; tel: 407-586-0000; www.gaylordpalms.com; $$$; map p.139 C1

As the name suggests, this is one of Orlando's best convention hotels, with a large amount of its sprawling grounds devoted to meeting spaces. Families may feel a bit out of their element here, but there is so much space you should be able to avoid the suits if need be. The 4.5-acre glass atrium recreates various destinations in Florida from St Augustine to Key West. The rooms carry on this theme. The **Canyon Ranch Spa** may be on site to help execs de-stress, but after a long vacation in Orlando

Prices for a standard double room:
$ under $100
$$ $100–$200
$$$ over $200

mom and dad may need to use its services as well.
SEE ALSO PAMPERING, P.96

Grand Cypress Resort
One Grand Cypress Boulevard, Orlando; tel: 407-239-1234; www.grandcypress.hyatt.com; $$$; map p.139 C4

This luxurious resort has a lush garden setting near Downtown Disney. Amenities include the famous **Grand Cypress Golf Academy** and four exclusive Jack Nicklaus-designed golf courses on property, a racquet club, windsurfing on the lake, a "Kids' Club," and an equestrian center, as well as convention facilities.
SEE ALSO GOLF, P.71

International Plaza Resort and Spa
10100 International Drive, Orlando; tel: 407-352-1100 or 800-327-0363; www.intlplaza resort.com; $$$; I-Ride: Greenline; map p.139 E4

This 17-story mock Spanish tower at the center of this sprawling hotel complex resembles an old Californian mission on growth hormones. Set in 28 acres of tropical landscaping, it has three pools and two kiddie pools, plus 60,000sq ft devoted to meeting spaces. And it's within walking distance of SeaWorld. Other amenities include three pools and miniature golf. A refrigerator and coffeemaker are in each room.

The Peabody Orlando
9801 International Drive, Orlando; tel: 407-352-4000 or 800-732-2639; www.peabody orlando.com; $$$; I-Ride: main and green lines; map p.136 A1

This 27-story landmark hotel in the tourist corridor has an Olympic-size pool and takes pride in being Orlando's convention hotel of choice. Though known for its twice-daily "March of the Peabody

Ducks," this is not really a place for kids. Guests looking for high tea and fine room service will feel more at home.

Perri House
10417 Vista Oaks Court, Lake Buena Vista; tel: 800-780-4830; www.perrihouse.com; $$; map p.139 C4

A chance to get away from it all without leaving the Disney area. This small country inn is secluded on a quiet 16-acre nature reserve adjacent to Walt Disney World,

Chain hotels and motels are both common and popular, but we have chosen not to cover them here in detail. Some people dislike chains because they offer no variety and lack a personal touch; on the other hand, once you have been to a hotel run by a particular chain, you can predict what kind of service and facilities to expect wherever else you are in the world. However, due to the intense competition in Orlando, especially at the budget end of the market, many chain hotels struggle to make much money here, and you may find that their facilities do not quite measure up to those in other areas. Below are the central reservation numbers and websites for some of the chains located near Disney:

La Quinta
Tel: 800-642-4271
www.lq.com

Marriott Courtyard
Tel: 888-236-2427
www.marriott.com

Comfort Suites
Tel: 877-424-6211
www.choicehotels.com

Holiday Inn
Tel: 800-465-4329
www.ichotelsgroup.com

Best Western
Tel: 800-780-7234
www.bestwestern.com

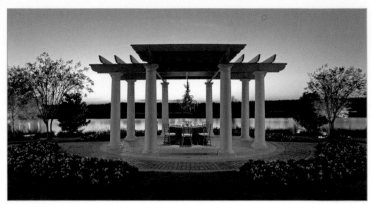

Above: The Ritz Carlton Grande Lakes is surrounded by exquisitely designed grounds.

and is a favorite of bird-watchers. The eight rooms are all individually decorated and have their own entrances and baths. The house has a communal library, kitchen, pool, and hot tub. Prices include a continental breakfast.

Renaissance Orlando Resort
6677 Sea Harbor Drive, Orlando; tel: 407-351-5555; www.renaissanceseaworld.com; $$$; I-Ride: mainline; map p.139 E4
This elegant 10-story tower and convention complex is perfect for business travelers as well as families. Rooms are huge and well appointed, and the service is first rate. A grand, sunlit atrium with sleek glass elevators and what appears to be acres of marble flooring encompass meeting facilities, waterfalls, goldfish ponds, and several shops and restaurants. A coffee shop and deli are good for a quick breakfast or lunch. The location is ideal for guests who want to explore several parks. The hotel is across the street from SeaWorld and Discovery Cove, and 15 minutes or less away from Universal Orlando and Disney World. Amenities

include a pool, an exercise room, a nearby spa, tennis courts, and more than 40 meeting rooms. All in all, it's great value in a prime location.

Ritz Carlton Orlando Grande Lakes
4012 Central Florida Parkway, Orlando; tel: 407-206-2400; www.ritzcarlton.com; $$$

Bed & breakfasts vary greatly in terms of price and quality, but the thing they have in common is that they are almost always in a private and/or historic homes. Few have restaurants, and the facilities will not be as good as in a regular hotel, but some travelers prefer the more personal ambience (and the often wonderful home-cooked breakfasts).

The Florida edition of the Charming Small Hotel Guides series published by Duncan Petersen is a good source for travelers wanting a personal touch. The Southeast edition of the Bed and Breakfast USA guide also lists B&Bs. Agencies specializing in finding B&B-style accommodations include: Bed & Breakfast Co. – Tropical Florida, tel: 305-661-3270, which covers the whole state.

Located to the east of International Drive, this luxury resort is designed to resemble a grand Italian *palazzo*. The rooms feature marble baths, are generously sized, and are impeccably appointed. Amenities include a 40,000sq-ft spa and a Greg Norman-designed golf course.

SEE ALSO GOLF, P.72

Rosen Shingle Creek
9939 Universal Boulevard, Orlando; tel: 866-996-9939 or 407-996-9939; www.shinglecreekresort.com; $$$; Link 58; map p.136 B1
This enormous resort seems to come out of nowhere. Though it is situated near I-Drive it stands alone and requires transportation to reach anything else. The rooms here are very well appointed and generously oversized compared to the average Orlando hotel room. Two fine restaurants, **Cala Bella** and **A Land Remembered** can keep guests more than happy on site. Among the other amenities are four heated pools, including a child's wading pool and a lap pool, the award-winning **Shingle Creek Golf Club,** and the **Shingle Creek Spa.**

Prices for a standard double room:
$ under $100
$$ $100–$200
$$$ over $200

Above: a garden guardian from the Courtyard at Lake Lucerne.

SEE ALSO GOLF, P.72–3; PAMPERING, P.97; RESTAURANTS, P.107–8

Sheraton Safari Hotel
12205 Apopka-Vineland Road, Orlando; tel: 407-239-0444 or 800-423-3297; www.sheraton safari.com; $$; map p.139 D3
This African-themed hotel has elaborate decor inside and out, with an over-the-top swimming pool that has a 79-ft python water slide, a lobby filled with indigenous sculpture, and animal print fabrics decorating every room. Free transportation to all Disney parks.

Wyndham Resort
8001 International Drive, Orlando; tel: 407-351-2420; www.wyndhamorlando resort.com; $$$; I-Ride: mainline; map p.136 A2
One of the best of the many choices along International Drive, this is a vast, sprawling and at times confounding place, yet it's surprisingly quiet, with more than 1,000 spacious rooms and pleasant swimming pools.

Downtown Orlando and Loch Haven Park

Courtyard at Lake Lucerne
211 North Lucerne Circle East, Orlando; tel: 407-648-5188; www.orlandohistoricinn.com; $$$; map p.135 C2
This is actually four B&Bs located alongside each other in Downtown Orlando. Three are fully restored historic houses, including a sprawling old plantation home; the fourth is Orlando's finest surviving Art Deco building. In all of the houses, the rooms are well appointed and have a welcoming air that you will never find in a hotel. Breakfast is, of course, included, as is a free cocktail in the evening.

Eö Inn
227 North Eola Drive, Orlando; tel: 407-481-8485; www.eoinn.com; $$$; map p.135 C2
This historic inn was built in 1923 and overlooks Lake Eola in the prestigious Thornton Park area. It was converted into a fine boutique hotel in 1999. With only 17 rooms, the service is always personable, and the decor is chic and spacious. With the **Urban Spa** on site, this hotel feels as much a retreat as a place to stay.
SEE ALSO PAMPERING, P.97

Veranda Bed & Breakfast
115 North Summerlin Avenue, Orlando; tel: 407-849-0321 or 800-420-6822; www.theveranda bandb.com; $$; map p.135 C2
What's this, a personalized retreat on a vacation in Orlando? Five cozy 1920s homes in downtown Orlando have been turned into this delightful B&B. All the rooms have hardwood floors and period furnishings. You couldn't find an experience further away from the anonymous chain hotels lining US 192 and I-Drive.

Westin Grand Bohemian Hotel
325 South Orange Avenue, Orlando; tel: 407-313-9000;

Below: the old-fashioned elegance of the Courtyard at Lake Lucerne.

Above: the rough and ready exterior of the Verannda B&B.

www.theboheme.com; $$$; map p.135 C2

This high-style, Bohemian-themed hotel, across from City Hall, calls itself "An Experience in Art and Music." More than 100 pieces of rare artwork, including drawings by Gustav Klimt and Egon Schiele, are displayed. The **Bösendorfer Lounge** offers nightly entertainment on one of only two Imperial Grand Bösendorfer pianos in the world. The 250 guest rooms and suites are dramatically furnished in dark Java wood tones, soft red and purple velvet fabrics, silver paint, Tiffany-style lamps, and the luxurious all-white Heavenly Bed. All rooms have CD players, high-speed internet access, three telephones (two with data ports), and interactive TV. The intimate

There is hardly a hotel or motel in all of central Florida that does not list "free transportation to Disney" as one of its amenities, but the services most provide are very limited, with one departure and one return from each park each day, hardly the way to a flexible vacation, especially with children.

and elegant four-star **Boheme Restaurant** attracts Downtown's business and arts community. Other amenities include a Starbucks coffee shop, heated outdoor pool, spa, massage room, workout room, and guest privileges at nearby Citrus Athletic Club.

SEE ALSO BARS AND CAFÉS, P.52; RESTAURANTS, P.109

Winter Park and Maitland

Park Plaza Hotel
307 Park Avenue South, Winter Park; tel: 407-647-1072; www.parkplazahotel.com; $$; map p.135 D4

This luxurious hotel is a bit off the beaten track for a Disney vacation, but exactly where you want to be to get away from a Disney vacation. Outside your door all the shopping and dining of Winter Park's Park Avenue awaits. Indoors, rooms are decorated with distinction in deep southern style and there is a garden restaurant to retreat to if you choose.

Thurston House Bed and Breakfast
851 Lake Avenue, Maitland; tel: 407-539-1911 or 800-843-2721; www.thurstonhouse.com; $$; Link 9; map p.30

Set on the shores of Lake

Eucalia, this Victorian farmhouse is a reminder of days long gone in central Florida. One thing that hasn't changed is you can still sit in a rocking chair on the veranda and watch the osprey dive for fish in the lake. The rooms have all the modern amenities you'd expect in a small hotel and some you wouldn't, such as original fireplaces filled with candles.

Space Coast

Cocoa Beach Oceanside Inn
1 Hendry Avenue, Cocoa Beach; tel: 321-784-3126; www.cocoa beachoceansideinn.com; $$

Forty rooms on the beach with a fantastic view of Cocoa Beach Pier and the Atlantic. Rooms have a clean, beachfront feel and the rooftop observation deck offers one of the best locations on the coast for watching launches from Kennedy Space Center. Other amenities include fishing, a pool, restaurant, and shuttle bus service.

Ron Jon Resort
1000 Shorewood Drive, Cape Canaveral; tel: 866-854-4835; www.ronjonresort.com; $$

Ron Jon has two quirky advantages: it is the closest oceanfront resort to most Orlando attractions and is the nearest place outside the Kennedy Space Center to watch a launch. This property is primarily for timeshare owners, but its unique locations makes it well worth checking out for a night or two on the coast. Kids will

Prices for a standard double room:
$ under $100
$$ $100–$200
$$$ over $200

Above: some vacation rentals can have as many as seven bedrooms, making them ideal for extended families to share.

love the elaborate pools, lazy river and water slide. The suites aren't big, but remain comfortable enough to accommodate a night or two.

Vacation Homes

You can hardly enter a shopping center along I-Drive or US 192 without encountering an office selling or renting vacation homes. Though similar, these should not be confused with timeshares.

Vaction homes are individually owned, but when owners' vacations do not require these houses or condos, the homes are offered through agencies to rent out to holidaymakers, hopefully at a profit for agency and homeowner alike.

Not only does this provide them with income, but it also means their property is regularly maintained and refurbished while they are away.

For guests this is an excellent opportunity to relax in a more welcoming environment than a hotel, and for bigger families this can mean big savings, as prices aren't much more expensive than the price for two hotel rooms.

Generally speaking these homes are located around US 192 in gated communities that have decent amenities themselves – from communal pools and tennis courts to internet services and tikki bars. Most homes will also have a private pool.

There is a downside to vacation rentals, in that it is difficult to know who you are dealing with and there can be a very large difference between the standards in properties. Do not make any arrangements without seeing pictures of the property and be very careful who you book your stay through.

VillaDirect Florida

6129 West Irlo Bronson Highway (US 192), Kissimmee; tel: 407-397-1210; www.villadirect.com
VillaDirect is a reliable internet-based company that has been providing vacation home rentals for several years. In addition to their local business, they also operate in Spain. Their service is unique in that they attempt to provide hotel-style services. Guests arrive at their main office to check in, receiving their keys, a welcome pack and further information. VillaDirect's maintanence teams keep all their properties clean and ready, and all are inspected prior to a customer's arrival. Their concierge service also arranges cots, high-chairs and any other items you may need, including groceries. Prices vary according to property sizes, which are anything from two-bed condos to six-bed houses.

Below: all vacation homes in Florida will have access to a pool.

Bars and Cafés

Orlando and the Disney resorts are hardly the first place that springs to mind when thinking of sophisticated drinking spots around the world, but there are still unique places to sit back and enjoy a drink. Disney and Universal's efforts tend to be highly themed, though the California Grill is a sophisticated retreat. British expats will find several "genuine" English pubs along I-Drive and US 192, but we've only listed the better ones here. If you want trendier options, head Downtown to places like the Bösendorfer Lounge and Sky 60. Wherever you go, remember to take a picture ID.

Animal Kingdom

Dawa Bar
Africa; map p.14
This is the only genuine bar in Disney's parks that does not serve food. Cocktails are served up with live contemporary African music and a beer brewed specially for Disney.

Disney Resorts

Big River Grille & Brewing Works
Disney's BoardWalk
Beer-lovers can sample a selection of handcrafted suds at Disney's first brewpub. The pub grub is nothing to write home about, but the outdoor seating is a good spot to sip a brew and watch the crowd pass by.

California Grill
Contemporary Resort
In many ways the luxuries of the Contemporary Resort have become dated, but one attraction that will never expire is its location; and the The California Grill's bar is a great place to have a drink during the fireworks at the Magic Kingdom.

Downtown Disney

Raglan Road Irish Pub and Restaurant
Pleasure Island; map p.92
Irish-owned and operated, this bar attempts an authentic re-creation of an Irish pub. They've succeeded if you're looking for the atmosphere of Dublin's Temple Bar during a tour group party; in other words it looks much like any other "authentic" Irish pub in America. Many shades of stout and ale are on offer alongside a fine selection of whiskey, and live Irish folk music takes you through the night. May the road rise to meet you.

Universal Studios

NASCAR Sports Grill

Universal Cineplex

Shops

Red Coconut Club

Pastamoré

Bob Marley- A Tribute to Freedom

PLAZA

Hard Rock Live

CityJazz

Pat O'Brien's Orlando

Hard Rock Cafe Orlando

Emeril's Restaurant Orlando

NBA City

the groove

Jimmy Buffet's Margaritaville

Latin Quarter

Islands of Adventure

CityWalk

Left: Finnegan's Bar and Grill at Universal Studios.

singalong crowd loves the dueling pianos, and foodies enjoy jambalaya, muffeletta, and other Big Easy specialties. Wash it down with a Hurricane, O'Brien's signature rum drink.

International Drive and Lake Buena Vista

Best of British Sports Bar and Grill

8324 International Drive, Orlando; tel: 407-264-9189; www.bobssoccerworld.com; daily 8am–late; I-Ride: mainline; map p.136 A2

People come here for one reason: the simple expat desire to watch European football and enjoy a decent pint, preferably together. Though the faux pub interior is not as good as some other expat crawls, you'll have no problem getting a pie and chips to watch the match and Stella, Carlsberg, and Guinness are all on tap.

Cricketers Arms

Festival Bay Mall, 5250 International Drive, Orlando; tel: 407-354-0686; www.cricketersarms pub.com; daily noon–2am; I-Ride: mainline; Link: 8, 24, 42; map p.136 B3

The epicenter of English expats and visitors caters to

Universal Studios

Finnegan's Bar and Grill

New York; map p.20

This full-service restaurant in New York also has a cozy Irish-style bar with Guinness and other Irish favorites on offer. Sports events are televised here if you need a distraction from the theme park around you. There is even a happy hour, something you'd never find at Disney.

Universal Studios Resorts

The Velvet Room

Hard Rock Hotel; 5800 Universal Boulevard, Orlando; tel: 407-503-2000; daily from 4pm; map p.136 A3

Music, whether it's a rocking soundtrack or live at the reservation-only Velvet Sessions, plays an unsurprisingly large part of the atmosphere at this chic cocktail bar. Chilled martinis are their signature drink, and appetizers are on offer to help line the stomach.

CityWalk

Pat O'Brien's Orlando

map p.50

An older crowd inhabits this replica of a landmark New Orleans watering hole. The

Below: The Velvet Room at the Hard Rock Hotel.

them with traditional ales and live football (known as soccer in these parts). Bar snacks include a chip butty and a cheese and Branston's pickle sandwich.

Downtown and Loch Haven Park

The Bösendorfer Lounge
Grand Bohemian Hotel, 325 South Orange Avenue, Orlando; tel: 407-313-9000; www.theboheme.com; daily; map p.135 C2

Enjoy the luxury of the Grand Bohemian Downtown without spending quite so much money. The Bösendorfer Lounge is named after the imperial grand piano that occupies it, making jazz nights very popular. There is a small food menu in the lounge, but the quality is as good as the hotel's main restaurant. Signature martinis, aged whiskies, and an impressive wine list comprise the tipple options.

The Celt Irish Pub
25 South Magnolia Avenue, Orlando; tel: 407-481-2928; www.harpandcelt.com; daily 11am–2am; map p.135 C2

Of course, any Irish pub is measured in the quality of its Guinness, and you can get a decent one here. Attached to **The Harp** restaurant, they also serve

good-quality pub grub here, with a selection of pies, Scotch eggs, and an Irish breakfast every Sunday from 11am–2pm. They show as much live rugby and soccer as they can, and on Saturday, fans of Notre Dame fill the pub during the college football season.

SEE ALSO RESTAURANTS, P.110

Church Street Bars
33–41 West Church Street, Orlando; tel: 407-649-4270; map p.134 C2

This is one building but includes three bars or a club to choose from. **Chillers** is undoubtedly the least inviting. Its cold atmosphere matches its frozen concoctions perfectly, and it's usually rather empty. Upstairs, **Latitudes** is a beach-themed rooftop bar inspired by Key West. The **Big Belly Brewery** believes in beer, beer, and more beer, though they do have spirits to wash it down with. Its comical wall hangings depict the effects of "Big Belly" syndrome on everyone from Captain Kirk to Bruce Springsteen. All of these places are meant for a drink with friends; go next door to **Antigua** when you're ready to rave.

SEE ALSO NIGHTLIFE, P.94

The Loaded Hog
19 North Orange Avenue, Wall Street Plaza, Orlando; tel: 407-649-1918; www.wallst plaza.com; daily 11am–2am; Link: 6, 7, 11, 13, 18, 51; map p.135 C2

This self-labeled watering hole has a cozier atmosphere than some of the more pretentious bars in the Wall Street Plaza complex. Happy-hour specials on margaritas and bottled beers.

The Monkey Bar
26 Wall Street Plaza, Orlando; tel: 407-481-1199; www.wallst plaza.com; daily 4pm–2am; Link: 6, 7, 11, 13, 18, 51; map p.135 C2

This might just be the classiest drinking den in the Wall Street Plaza, with a sedate interior and a balcony overlooking the hectic scene below. Oversized martinis are their specialty – drink with caution. Happy-hour specials on cocktails.

One Eyed Jack's
15 North Orange Avenue, Wall Street Plaza, Orlando; tel: 407-648-2050; www.wallst plaza.com; daily 11am–2am; Link: 6, 7, 11, 13, 18, 51; map p.135 C2

This dark little bar aims itself at serious drinkers. Spin its drink wheel and slurp what you're given. Happy-hour specials on margaritas and bottled beers.

Sky 60
54 North Orange Avenue, Orlando; tel: 407-648-5441; www.sky60.com; Wed–Sat 8pm–2am; Link: 6, 7, 11, 13, 18, 51; map p.135 C2

This rooftop bar is minimalist to the core: with a concrete floor, slim bar, and white curtained cabanas providing privacy. It attracts a creative crowd with airs, but offers a fine view of the everyday world below.

Below: real ale and real football are frequently served.

Above: Fiddler's Green's courtyard.

The Tuk Tuk Room
25 Wall Street Plaza, Orlando; tel: 407-849-9904; www.wallst plaza.com; daily 11am–2am; Link: 6, 7, 11, 13, 18, 51; map p.135 C2

The tiny bar's decor is based on an Indonesian beach bar, and the happy-hour specials include sushi rolls.

Waitiki
26 Wall Street Plaza, Orlando; tel: 407-481-1199; www.wallst plaza.com; daily 11am–2am; Link: 6, 7, 11, 13, 18, 51; map p.135 C2

This retro tiki lounge has mojitos in 10 different flavors, a few frozen drinks and other alcoholic concoctions consistent with its Caribbean holiday theme. Seafood snacks and sandwiches are served until 11pm. Happy-hour specials make the mojitos so cheap you could dare to try them all.

Wall Street Cantina
11 North Orange Avenue, Wall Street Plaza, Orlando; tel: 407-420-1515; www.wallst plaza.com; daily 11am–2am; Link: 6, 7, 11, 13, 18, 51; map p.135 C2

Known for their notorious collection of margaritas (one comes with a strict two-per-person limit), the Cantina also serves a good selection of Tex-Mex food that can be accompanied by a bucket of beer if you choose. Happy-hour specials on margaritas and Corona beer.

Winter Park

Austin's Coffee
929 West Fairbanks Avenue, Winter Park; tel: 407-975-3364; www.austinscoffee.com; Mon–Thur 7am–11pm, Fri and Sat 7am–1am, Sun 8am–midnight; Link: 1, 9, 13; map p.135 D4

> Prepare to be flattered when ordering a drink in Orlando. You could be collecting your retirement pension and still be "carded" at the bar, as many bars will ask to see everyone's ID before allowing them an alcoholic drink no matter what your age. They may even refuse you service if you are unable to produce proof you are over 21.

Walk into Austin's on a weekday and their prime customer becomes immediately obvious: studious college kids from Rollins take over entire booths with laptops, notes, books, and coffee. At night the mood relaxes, with events including poetry slams and open mic nights. In addition to organic, fair-trade coffee they sell beer, wine, and various teas.

Fiddler's Green
544 West Fairbanks Avenue, Winter Park; tel: 407-645-2050; www.fiddlersgreenorlando.com; Mon–Sat 11am–2am, Sun 11am–12am; Link: 1, 9; map p.135 D4

Though Fiddler's Green is a healthy walk away from Rollins College, that doesn't keep the students away from its traditional Irish fare. In addition to the standard drinks of Guinness, Murphy's and Harp, there are several imported European beers on tap. Hearty food such as bangers and mash and shepherd's pie are available for lunch and dinner. Pints are a buck cheaper at happy hour.

Behind the Scenes

Disney and SeaWorld offer some unique opportunities to get "backstage" and see the inner workings of these enormous theme parks. The chance to interact with the dolphins and whales at SeaWorld and Epcot are once-in-a-lifetime affairs. The other tours offer access to areas of the park off limits to most guests and provide an insight into their creation and operation. The prices given below are for the tours only and do not include the cost of the day's ticket unless stated. Bookings for all of these tours must be made well in advance of arrival as their numbers are strictly limited.

Magic Kingdom
Family Magic
Two-and-a-half hours; $27; must be three or older

This tour amounts to not much more than an elaborate scavenger hunt at the Magic Kingdom. Before booking, consider whether your kids are really going to want to maintain this gimmick for over two hours when all around them thrill rides and shows are waiting. No special access included.

Keys to the Kingdom
Five hours; $60; must be 16 or older

There is so much to do at the Magic Kingdom that it is easy to forget what a novelty it was at the time of creation. This tour takes visitors to significant sights, both in the park and backstage, to tell the story of Walt's original vision and numerous, humorous anecdotes about the park's creation.

The Magic Behind Our Steam Trains
Three hours; $40; must be 10 or older

Prior to the park opening, you are given access to the backstage roundhouse where Disney stores its vintage steam trains and get the chance to go along with the engineers as they prepare them for the day ahead. A unique opportunity for trainspotters.

Mickey's Magical Milestones
Two hours; $25; must be nine or older

This tour of the park traces the development of Mickey Mouse himself, from original doodles and the first feature *Steamboat Willie* to the latest 3-D experience of Mickey's PhilharMagic.

Epcot
Backstage Magic
Seven hours; $199; Must be 16 or older; lunch at Mama Melrose's Ristorante Italiano included

Though this tour begins at Epcot, you also visit Hollywood Studios and the Magic Kingdom to discover just how Disney's special effects are created.

Behind the Seeds
One hour; $14 for over tens, $10 for nine and under; must be three or older

For budding gardeners of any age, this tour explores in further detail the hydroponic gardens you briefly see on the Living with the Land ride.

DiveQuest
Three hours, water time is only 40 minutes; $140; must be 10 or older and in possession of scuba certification

A more in-depth chance to explore the Nemo aquarium than the Seas Aqua Tour. The time in the water is a bit longer and full scuba equipment is provided in the cost, allowing you greater access than the snorkelers above.

> To book any of the Disney behind-the-scenes experiences, tel: 407-939-8687. Places on these excursions are limited, so you need to make your reservation well in advance to avoid disappointment.

> There are more tours available at SeaWorld than we have space to list here. For more information or to make a booking, tel: 800-327-2424.

Left: getting to know the Beluga.

A rare chance to get in the water with a Beluga whale. Only a few places are available each day, and each group is accompanied by trainers who teach you to communicate with this intelligent Arctic creature.

Marine Mammal Keeper

All day from 6.30am; $399; must be 13 or older

This experience lasts the entire day and takes you backstage to accompany trainers and carers as they prepare meals for Sea-World's wildlife. You also get up close to the sealife during feeding times. The price includes a seven-day pass to SeaWorld.

Sharks Deep Dive

Two hours; $150; must be 10 or older

Participants on this tour get the dubious pleasure of being locked in a cage and then submerged into an aquarium full of hungry sharks, while being watched by hungry diners at the Underwater Grille. A special helmet provides air and is equipped with a microphone so you can speak with your cohorts underwater.

Dolphins in Depth

Three hours; $150; must be 13 or older

This tour gives you a chance to have a close-up encounter in shallow water with a dolphin resident at the Nemo and Friends aquarium. Not as nice an encounter as the experience at Discovery Cove *(see p.121–2)*, but much cheaper.

Seas Aqua Tour

Two-and-a-half hours, water time is only 30 minutes; $100; must be eight or older

A chance to explore the aquarium at the Seas with Nemo and Friends from the inside, gaining a closer look at the 65 species of fish and dolphin who live there. Snorkeling only.

Animal Kingdom

Backstage Safari

Three hours; $65; must be 16 or older

This walking safari offers more than just special access to the animals; it also includes time with the staff who are responsible for everything from toucans to tigers. A singular opportunity to learn about the special challenges the carers face on a daily basis.

Wild by Design

Three hours; $58; must be 14 or older

Anyone who has ridden on Kilimanjaro Safaris will appreciate that Disney has created a unique "zoo" experience that appears as natural and free as the real thing. This tour reveals just how the secrets behind this design were concealed.

SeaWorld

Beluga Interaction

Two hours; $179; must be 10 or older

Below: the fine design and engineering of Disney's Animal Kingdom is the subject of Backstage Safari.

Budgeting and Survival

Taking on Orlando's theme parks can be a daunting prospect, especially with young children. The crowds, the heat, and the outlandish prices can sap your strength and empty your wallet before you know what's hit you. But it doesn't have to be that way. If you think things through before leaving home and arrive prepared you can save time, energy, and, most importantly, money. So, in the interest of mental and financial health, here are a few tips to prevent your dream vacation from turning into a nightmare.

Budgeting for Your Trip

HOTELS

If you're looking for a hotel with an acceptable minimum level of comfort, cleanliness, and facilities, a reasonable starting point for the price of a double room is $50 in budget-class hotels. Going up from there to around $80 should make a significant difference in quality. For between $100 and $150 a whole array of hotels opens up, ranging from bland business-traveler places to characterful establishments.

If you are staying at Disney, there is a world of difference between their budget and moderate resort categories, not to mention the deluxe options. At the budget resorts themes are high, but costs are cut; food options are poor at best and rooms cramped.

When you pay to move up a level, the facilities improve dramatically. Pools have excellent themes, slides and bars; restaurants serve tasty food, room service is good quailty, kids' activities are better, and the staff are always on hand to help. If you want to enjoy the best of Disney, go deluxe or moderate.

FOOD

Food costs range from a few dollars for a bagel and coffee, through $25–40 for a 2–3-course meal at a standard (often chain) restaurant. Really special fare begins at $40 and a fine restaurant can be as pricey as you can handle.

TRANSPORTATION

Getting around by Disney transport and hotel shuttles to the park is free. Lynx buses cost $1.50, and taxis, due to the distance inherent in most journeys through Orlando, are expensive. Expect to spend at least $30.

Home Suite Home

Staying in a room with a kitchenette at Disney can be a costly affair, but off-resort on US 192 or I-Drive you will find many hotels that offer this valuable extra for families at a reasonable price. Not only will cooking meals at home save money in the long term, it also provides that "normal" family downtime for kids and adults to unwind after a hectic day.

Readmission

Though all theme parks sell admission for an entire day, each has its own regulations for those wishing to return to a park already visited that day. Ask a member of staff as you leave. Some will require you to have a hand stamp while others are happy simply to see your ticket again later.

Student Travelers

If you're looking to do Orlando on the cheap, you can succeed so long as you keep your expectations realistic. During the low season many budget hotels can have very affordable rates (especially if sharing), and transportation to Disney or Universal is available via Lynx, so long as you plan well. Food purchased outside the park can be inexpensive. And though there is no way to avoid paying a lot for your

It's a rare family that tours a theme park unscathed. The ones who have the most fun, while enduring the fewest minor hassles and outright meltdowns, are those who remember the cardinal rule of theme-park touring: slow down. This is a vacation, remember?

Another option is to rent one of the numerous vacation homes available through companies like **VillaDirect** – an ideal solution for larger families.
SEE ALSO ACCOMMODATIONS, P.49

Ticketing

There is an enormous variety of tickets offered at both Universal Studios and Walt Disney World Parks. Disney guests traveling from the US or purchasing tickets on the day of arrival can buy a one-day, one-park pass for about $65, or a Park Hopper pass that allows you access to more than one park and

ranges in price from $95 for one day to $250 for 10 days.

Disney's Magic Your Way ticket allows you to customize your park options. The base ticket runs from 1–10 days and costs from $60 for one day to $187 for 10. You can add the Park Hopper Option for about $50 to allow you to visit more than one park in a single day. Additionally, you can add a certain number of visits to other attractions like Blizzard Beach and the Wide World of Sports for $53.25, and if you wish to keep your tickets from expiring, you can pay $20 so that all unused days can be used on your next visit. Otherwise, they will all expire 14 days after their first use.

Universal Studios have a more straightforward approach with a two-day, two-park ticket with the third day free costing $57, but team up with SeaWorld and Wet'n Wild to offer 14-day passes from $139. They also regularly offer special deals on the website www.universal studios.com.

Above: Universal Express eliminates waiting in line. It's free for hotel guests, but costly for those staying off-resort.

entry tickets, once inside there is no need to spend a penny. **The Palm Lakefront Hostel** is the only hostel near the parks.
SEE ALSO ACCOMMODATIONS, P.42

Curb Your Enthusiasm

It's difficult to resist the hype surrounding Orlando's theme parks, but consider the hazards of trying to do too much. Unrealistic expectations will lead only to disappointment and exhaustion. Forget about packing as much as possible into your visit, or even following some preordained schedule. Instead, select three or four "must-dos" for each day and fill in with other attractions as time allows. Remember, if you find yourself feeling more stressed-out than at a typical day of work, you are probably missing the point.

The second most important rule is to use your time wisely. The key here is to visit the parks at the least crowded time of day, which in almost all cases is first thing in the morning.

Arrive at the parks about an hour before the posted opening. That way you can park, buy a ticket, and enter as soon as the gates swing open. Parks at Disney World and Universal Orlando usually open at least 30 minutes prior to the official time, although all attractions may not yet be running. You can often do more in the first two hours, when lines are short and temperatures are mild, than in the remainder of the afternoon. Attendance peaks between 11am and 4pm – a good time for meals, shopping, and less popular attrac-

> Though it is wisest to save your theme-park purchases for the way home, if you see something you just can't resist at any Disney World shop you can ask for your purchase to be held for you at Package Pickup near City Hall at Town Square. This will keep you from lugging your purchases around all day. Additionally, you can ask for purchases to be delivered to your hotel if you are staying on-resort.

tions. If you're staying at an on-site resort, you might even sneak back to your hotel for a swim and a snooze. Keep in mind also that the Disney parks stop selling tickets when they reach capacity – another inducement to stake your claim early.

Park Opening Hours

Knowing the time a park opens is not as easy as it sounds. Opening hours at all Orlando parks are calculated on a complex matrix that attempts to maximize the use of park staff and other resources. This makes for such a complicated and unpredictable schedule that you are strongly advised to consult the parks shortly before visiting.

The easiest way is via the Web; www.disneyworld.com and www.universalorlando.com provide up-to-date information on hours and entertainment schedules. For those without Web access, telephone Disney on 407-939-6244 or Universal on 407-363-8000.

> Most visitors can expect to walk 4 to 8 miles in a typical day at a theme park.

FASTPASS

The biggest gripe people have about visiting theme parks is the long lines. Both Disney and Universal have heard your grumbles and now offer several programs that greatly reduce the amount of time you'll spend staring at the back of another person's head.

The FASTPASS system allows you to collect a timed ticket for parks' most popular attractions. As the day goes on the time between ticket issue and redemption continues to grow. Some rides, such as Space Mountain, may run out of FASTPASS tickets before lunchtime. Though it is down to the discretion of the cast member, expired FASTPASSes are usually accepted.

You are allowed to hold two "waiting" FASTPASSes at any time so long as they are for different rides. As soon as your FASTPASS window for a particular attraction begins you are no longer considered to be "waiting", and you can collect another FASTPASS for any attraction, even if you have yet to use your initial FASTPASS.

PhotoPass

There is little point in "having a magical day" without photographic evidence. Disney's PhotoPass system is a mixed blessing. For those who do not feel adept at the use of a camera, and, it must be said, have a substantial amount of money to burn, purchasing this pass gives you access to dozens of professional photographers stationed throughout the park ready to take your perfect picture. Once you return home you can view all of your pictures online and receive prints, scrapbooks, and various other products.

When to Visit

Plan your visit to Orlando very carefully. Visiting during the least crowded seasons usually makes for a far more pleasant experience at the theme parks. Crowds and waiting times are daunting during the busy seasons. The obvious times to avoid are those coinciding with American school vacations. During the summer break (mid-June to late August), spring break and Easter periods (March/April), and Thanksgiving or Christmas, you will encounter the heaviest crowds and priciest hotel rooms.

From September until Thanksgiving, crowds are light, as they are in January and between the holiday weekends of Thanksgiving and Christmas.

The Sun

The Florida sun is unmerciful, so wear light-colored clothing, a hat and sunglasses, and use plenty of sunscreen. It is vital during the summer months that you retreat indoors frequently. This could even be as often as every hour. Shops and restaurants are always nice and cool, and no one will mind if you are just browsing or sitting down to drink your own bottle of water. Live shows and indoor attractions are a great escape as well.

Below: occasionally try to remind yourself you're on vacation.

Children

For Orlando, one chapter devoted to children's activities is hardly enough – you need an entire book. So we've planted tips throughout in an effort to help families on vacation. Here we try to point out some of the better attractions for various age groups. Our hope is that this will help kids, no matter what their age, get even more pleasure out of the parks, which will of course let the parents get more pleasure out of their kids. Those with children between the ages of five and 12 will have the easiest times. Under-fives are still well catered for, though teenagers may find dealing with mom and dad all day a price too high, even for Disney.

Under-5s

THEME PARKS...
The Magic Kingdom is the best theme park for the younger kids. Its dark rides, such as **Peter Pan's Flight** and **it's a small world**, are a big hit with the smallest of fans but can be a bit too tedious for those who've outgrown the characters they feature. Said characters are especially entertaining at character dining experiences held at Cinderella's Castle and Crystal Palace, amongst other locations. Check times when entering parks.

Islands of Adventures' **Seuss Landing** and Universal Studios' **Woody Woodpecker's Kidzone** are both brilliant jungle gyms by any other name.

Unexpectedly, many tots find most of the 3-D attractions in Orlando a bit too terrifying, as some sort of bug

Most thrill rides at all parks now have parent swap stations so that couples with children can all wait in the line for a ride and then take turns riding it.

Above: a hug worth waiting for.

scampering up your legs is a standard gag. Plus, the graphics can be so realistic they may forget that it's just a film. The one possible exception to this is **Mickey's PhilharMagic** in the Magic Kingdom, which is just as entertaining as other films, but suitable for all ages.
SEE ALSO MAGIC KINGDOM, P.6–9; UNIVERSAL STUDIOS, P.21; ISLANDS OF ADVENTURE, P.22

...AND BEYOND
If seeing animatronic animals or those in captivity leaves your child wanting more, the

Green Meadows Petting Farm gives kids the chance to milk a cow, ride a pony, go on a hay ride, and get up close to over 200 animals.
SEE ALSO NATURAL WORLD, P.90

5–12

THEME PARKS...
Hollywood Studios and **Animal Kingdom** are the most appealing Disney Parks for those young children who want to relive the adventures of movies and see wildlife, but are still a bit too timid for thrill rides.

Don't forget to take along an autograph book and pen to gather lasting memories of character greetings. The compulsion to collect can also be quenched by trading pins at stalls located throughout the Disney resort.

Stunt shows such as **Indiana Jones Epic Stunt Spectacular** at Hollywood Studios are great for those too big to be scared by noise but not big enough to see through the stunts' illusions (and they are performed in shaded pavilions and last long enough for you to get a bit of a rest).

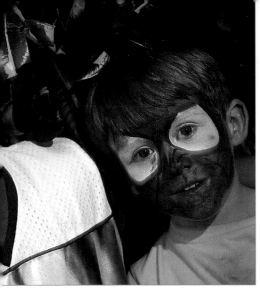

Left: superheroes in the making.

Test Track and **Mission: SPACE**, but the other exhibits are likely to bore even the most inquisitive adolescent.

As far as nightlife goes, **CityWalk** and **Downtown Disney** both provide a safe environment for teens to mingle (and get away from their parents).

Though entrance is expensive, the amusements at **DisneyQuest** could entertain a teen for the entire day (or evening) and there are plenty of places nearby (**House of Blues** just across the street) that could allow adults the comfort of mind and the relaxing beverages needed after a long day at the parks.

SEE ALSO EPCOT, P.10–3; DISNEY–MGM STUDIOS, P.16–7; ISLANDS OF ADVENTURE, P.22–3; NIGHTLIFE, P.93; THEMED ATTRACTIONS, P.120

...AND BEYOND
For those desperate to get behind the wheel of a car, **Fun Spot Action Park** provides bumper cars and four multilevel tracks for go-cart racing.
SEE ALSO THEMED ATTRACTIONS, P.119

All hotels will provide cots and other items needed for children, often at no extra cost. Disney Resorts also offer childcare for when parents want to have a night away and many hotels off-resort offer affordable suites designed for young families.

It may be impossible to pull kids away from **Discovery Cove**, where you get a handshake and a kiss from a dolphin before it swims you back to shore. It's something most children could only dream of. The park is exceptionally expensive, but travel agents often offer specials and the memory is irreplaceable.
SEE ALSO ANIMAL KINGDOM, P.14–5; HOLLYWOOD STUDIOS, P.16–7; THEMED ATTRACTIONS, P.121

...AND BEYOND
If you've got a young one whose taste for the disgusting and bizarre seems insatiable, **Ripley's Believe It or Not! Odditorium** may be just the place for them. Exhibits include a two-headed calf, among other oddities.

Really for all ages, the

Orlando Science Center is a must-see, with interactive exhibits covering everything from life in zero gravity to a journey through the human body.
SEE ALSO MUSEUMS AND GALLERIES, P.84; THEMED ATTRACTIONS, P.118

Teens

THEME PARKS...
Assuming your teen wants to push the limits of motion sickness, Universal's Islands of Adventure with the **Incredible Hulk** and **Dueling Dragons** roller coasters, plus the **Amazing Adventures of Spider Man** and other disorientating rides should be top of their list. Hollywood Studios, thanks to the **Twilight Zone Tower of Terror** and the **Rock 'n' Roller Coaster**, is the next best stop. Epcot has two fantastic thrill rides in

---

In the parks, walking distances are quite long, but strollers are available for rent. The sun, heat, and humidity can take their toll, especially during long waits for popular attractions.

Below: even younger children still find Disney a magical place.

Essentials

Orlando and the theme parks are easy to negotiate. Disney especially makes travel carefree. You could in theory be taken from airport to resort and back again and never leave Disney's safe hands. For those wanting a bit more independence, here is all the practical information you need on how to get yourself into the country, what to do in an emergency, how to understand the currency, and where to find the tourist offices. There are also details on health care, telecommunications, and where to leave your dog. For additional information, visit the useful the websites listed on pages 65–6.

Business Hours

Off-resort, most businesses are open 9am–5pm, with many of the shopping malls open as late as 10pm. Many large supermarkets and numerous restaurants stay open 24 hours.

Banks usually remain open until at least 4pm from Monday through Thursday, and until 6pm on Friday. Some banks are open for a short time on Saturday.

Below: as beautiful as it is, Florida leads the US in the frequency of lightning storms.

During some public holidays, some or all state, local, and federal agencies may be closed. Local banks, businesses, stores, and attractions may also stop operating during some public holidays.

Climate Hazards

TORNADOES
Florida ranks eighth in the list of US states with the most tornadoes per year, but they're not nearly as bad as the awesome twisters that assail the Midwest. Trailer parks are particularly vulnerable.

LIGHTNING
Florida is unofficially dubbed the "lightning capital of the country." This is attributed to the hot, wet air that lies close to the ground, and unstable atmospheric conditions that exist mainly from May until September.

If you see dark clouds and flashes of lightning approaching, take cover. If in a car, stay inside until the storm passes. If in a building, don't "make a run for it." Many lightning victims are killed when getting into or out of their cars.

Walt Disney World is in a state of its own. It administers its own planning, has the power to build roads and water systems, and runs its own police and fire-fighting forces. It even has the approval to construct a nuclear power plant, should it ever find this a necessity.

Boaters should head for the nearest place they can tie up and evacuate the boat. During any nearby lightning storm, parks will close their outdoor attractions.

Customs Regulations

You will be given a form to complete en route to the US that requires basic identification information. When landed, you must go to an inspection area where a CBP (Customs and Border Protection) Officer will determine why you are coming to the US, if you have the necessary documents, and how long you intend to stay. If you are allowed to proceed, your passport and customs declaration form will be stamped.

Left: pack a raincoat in Autumn, as sudden downpours are frequent.

from your nearest US Embassy or Consulate or on the US Customs website: see above. Other useful links are listed below.

US Department of Homeland Security
www.dhs.gov/trip
Transportation Security Administration
www.tsa.gov/travelers

CUSTOMS ALLOWANCES
Articles brought into the United States are subject to duty or internal revenue tax. Visitors, however, are given an allowance of exempted goods. These include:

Money. There is no limit on the amount of money – US or foreign traveler's checks or money orders – that you may bring into or take out of the US. But you must declare amounts exceeding $10,000 or the foreign currency equivalent.

Alcohol. Visitors over the age of 21 are permitted to bring in 34fl oz of alcohol for their personal use. Excess quantities are subject to duty and tax.

Cigars and cigarettes. Visitors may bring in not more than 200 cigarettes (one

Hand in the return part (departure record) of the form filled out en route to the country when you leave the country (the cbp officer should have attached it to your passport on arrival. Failure to do so will cause you problems with the CBP in the future.
US Customs and Border Protection
www.cbp.gov

PROHIBITED GOODS
Articles which visitors are forbidden to take into the United States include: Liquor-filled chocolates or candy, dangerous drugs, obscene publications, hazardous articles (e.g. fireworks), and narcotics.

Travelers using medicines containing narcotics (such as tranquilizers or cough medicine) should carry a prescription and/or a note from their doctor, and should take only the quantity required for a short stay. The medicine must be in its original, clearly labelled container. The medication must also be able to be legally prescribed in the US.

Meat and poultry, fruit and veg, most dairy, absinthe, more than 250 grams caviar, and Cuban cigars are all prohibited.

Any liquids, gels, and aerosols in carry-on luggage must be in 3oz containers or smaller. These must be placed in a quart-size, zip-top, clear plastic bag – one per traveler.

There are exceptions for prescription and over-the-counter medicines and baby formula. Put larger amounts (e.g. shampoo) in luggage.

Full details of customs requirements are available

Below: be patient at customs and immigration; waits are common.

Above: machine-readable passports are compulsory if issued after 26 October 2006.

carton), 50 cigars (as long as they are not Cuban), or 3lbs of smoking tobacco, or proportionate amounts of each. An additional 100 cigars may be brought in under your gift exemption.

Gifts. As a visitor to the US, you can claim on entry up to $100 worth of merchandise, free of duty and tax, as gifts for other people. Such articles may have to be inspected, so do not gift-wrap them until after you have entered the country.

Disabled Travelers

Accessibility and facilities are excellent at the theme parks and other attractions in Orlando. Special parking is available near the entrances to each park, the hotels, and other facilities.

Wheelchairs are available for rent in limited numbers in several locations, usually outside or just inside the entrance. For some attractions and rides, guests may remain in wheelchairs. For others, they must be able to leave the wheelchair. Regulations are clearly indicated in leaflets and at the appropriate entrance. Some motorized wheelchairs are available for rent, and nearly all buses and launches can accommodate conventional wheelchairs. Wheelchair access is available at toilets in all the theme parks.

For hearing-impaired guests, there is a TDD at City Hall in Magic Kingdom, at Guest Services in Hollywood Studios, Epcot and Animal Kingdom, and at both Universal parks. Many rides and attractions have closed captioning. A sign-language interpreter is available for theater shows.

Sight-impaired guests can borrow complimentary cassettes and tape recorders at the same locations. A deposit is required.

Electricity

110–115 volts; flat two- or three-pronged plugs.

Embassies and Consulates

Few English-speaking countries have a consulate in Florida. These are the nearest ones to contact:

Australia
2103 Coral Way, Suite 108, Miami, FL 33145; tel: 305-858-7633

British Consulate
200 South Orange Avenue, Suite 2110, Orlando, FL 32801; tel: 407-426-7855; map p.132 C2

Canada Consulate General
200 South Biscayne Boulevard, Suite 1600, Miami, Florida 33131; tel: 305-579-1600

New Zealand
Embassy, 37 Observatory Circle, NW, Washington DC 20008; tel: 202-328-4800

Republic of Ireland
345 Park Avenue, 17th Floor, New York, NY 10022; tel: 212-319-2555

South Africa
333 East 38th Street, 9th Floor, New York, NY 10016; tel: 212-213-4880

Entry Requirements

Most foreign visitors need a machine-readable passport (which should be valid for at least six months longer than their intended stay) and a visa to enter the United States. You should also be able to provide evidence that you intend to leave the United States after your visit is over (usually in the form of a return or onward ticket), and visitors from some countries need an international vaccination certificate.

Certain foreign nationals are exempt from the normal visa requirements. Canadian citizens with a valid Canadian passport need no visa. Nor do Mexican citizens provided

> Note that immigration officials are entitled to ask for proof of solvency on your arrival in the United States. You will also be fingerprinted and have an iris scan in immigration.

they have a Mexican passport and a US Border Crossing Card (Form I-186 or I-586), and as long as they are residents of Mexico.

A special "visa-waiver" program means that citizens of some countries do not require a visa if they are staying for less than 90 days and have a round-trip or onward ticket. These include New Zealand, Japan, the UK, and about 18 other European nations. If you travel under this program, you will need to present an e-passport if your passport was assigned on or after 26 October 2006.

Mistakes are not accepted on immigration forms you fill in during the flight. So don't cross anything out – ask for a new form.

Those requiring a visa or visa information can apply by mail or by personal application to their local US Embassy or Consulate.

Vaccination certificate requirements vary, but proof of immunization against smallpox or cholera may be necessary.

Etiquette

LIQUOR LAWS
The legal drinking age in Florida is 21. Liquor can be purchased on any day of the week, but note that some municipalities do not permit retail stores to sell liquor until after 1pm on Sundays.

SMOKING
Smoking is not permitted on any attraction, ride, or in any waiting area in theme parks. Furthermore, smoking is banned in all public places in Florida. This includes bars, restaurants, and cafés. Some hotels still offer smoking

rooms, but the number is dwindling.

Health and Medical Care
You should never leave home without travel insurance to cover both yourself and your belongings. Your own insurance company or travel agent can advise you on policies, but shop around, since rates vary. Make sure you are covered for accidental death, emergency medical care, trip cancelation, and baggage or document loss.

MEDICAL CARE
In the event you need medical assistance, ask the reception staff at your hotel. The larger resort hotels may well have a resident doctor.

There is nothing cheap about being sick in the US, whether it involves a simple visit to the doctor or a spell in a hospital. The initial ER fee charged by a good hospital might be $250, and that's before the additional cost of X-rays, medicines, and so on have been added. It is therefore essential to be armed with adequate medical insurance, and to carry an identification card or policy number at all times.

Above: kennels at parks help keep "best friends" happy.

No Smoking Please

Above: it's the law.

HEALTH HAZARDS
The two most common health hazards in Orlando are sunburn and heat exhaustion; both are easily avoided.

The heat alone can be a danger, especially for the elderly or those with a pre-existing medical condition. Dehydration and salt deficiency can lead to heat exhaustion. The main symptoms are headache, weakness, lightheadedness, muscle aches, cramps, and agitation. Make a point of drinking plenty of non-alcoholic fluids (before you get thirsty), and take periodic breaks in the shade or an air-conditioned environment.

If untreated, heat exhaustion can escalate to a far more serious case of heatstroke, which means that the body's temperature rises to dangerous levels. In addition to the symptoms listed above, people suffering from heatstroke may exhibit confusion, strange behavior, and even seizures. If you suspect a companion is suffering from heatstroke, get them to a cool place, apply cold damp cloths, and call for a doctor immediately.

Internet

Walt Disney World
http://disneyworld.disney.go.com
Universal Studios
www.universalstudios.com

Above: the US is slowly doing away with its one size and color fits all denominations.

SeaWorld
www.seaworld.com
Busch Gardens
www.buschgardens.com
Orlando Visitors Bureau
www.orlandoinfo.com
Florida Tourist Board
www.visitflorida.com
Golf in Orlando
www.golforland.com
Hotel Discounts
www.orlandohoteldiscounts.com
Restaurants in Orlando
http://orlando.diningguide.net
Orlando Nightlife
www.orlando.nightguide.com
Kennedy Space Center
www.ksc.nasa.gov

Kennels

All theme parks provide kennels for those guests who are traveling with canine companions – sorry, no dogs on Space Mountain.

Money

Foreign visitors are advised to take US dollar travelers' checks or cash to Orlando, since exchanging foreign currency – whether as cash or checks – can prove problematic. An increasing number of banks, including the First Union National Bank, Nations Bank, and Sun Bank chains, offer foreign exchange facilities, but this practice is not universal. Some department stores offer foreign currency exchange.

Most shops and restaurants accept travelers' checks in US dollars and will give change in cash. Alternatively, checks can be converted into cash at the bank.

Credit cards are very much part of daily life in Orlando and can be used to pay for pretty much anything, and it is also common for car rental firms and hotels to take an imprint of your card as a deposit. Rental companies may oblige you to pay a large deposit in cash if you do not have a card.

You can also use your credit or bank cards to withdraw cash from ATMs. Before you leave home, make sure you know your PIN number and find out which ATM system will accept your card. The most widely accepted cards are Visa, American Express, MasterCard, Diners Club, Japanese Credit Bureau, and Discover. Maestro cards are often not accepted.

Be sure to check the rate of exchange and any other charges your financial institution may levy before using your card abroad. Some charge prohibitive rates.

> Most theme parks have locker rental at the entrance. Charges vary but they are invariably useful.

TIPPING

Service personnel expect tips in Orlando. The accepted rate for baggage handlers in airports is at least $1 per bag. For others, including taxi drivers and waiters, 15–20 percent is the going rate, depending on the level and quality of service. Sometimes tips are included in restaurant bills when dining in groups.

Moderate hotel tipping is around 50 cents per bag or suitcase handled by porters or bellboys. You should tip a doorman if he holds your car or performs other services. It is not necessary to tip chamber staff unless you stay several days.

Postal Services
POST OFFICES
The opening hours of post offices vary between central, big-city branches and those in smaller towns or suburbs, but all open Monday to Friday and some open on Saturday mornings.

Drugstores and hotels usually have a small selection of stamps, and there are stamp-vending machines in some transport terminals.

DELIVERY SERVICES
For the best service, you should pay for Express Mail

via the US postal service, which guarantees next-day delivery within the US and delivery in two to three days to foreign destinations. Privately owned courier services, which offer next-day delivery to most places, are also very popular.

Telephone numbers for the main courier services are:

FedEx: 800-463-3339
DHL: 800-225-5435
UPS: 800-742-5877

Tourist Information Offices

Below is a list of tourist information offices in and around Orlando.

ORLANDO
Orlando/Orange County Convention and Visitors Bureau
8723 International Drive, Suite 101, Orlando 32819; tel: 407-363-5872; www.orlando info.com; I-Ride: mainline; map p.136 A1
Walt Disney World Co
1800 Epcot Resort Boulevard, Lake Buena Vista, 32830; tel: 407-939-6244; www.walt disneyworld.com
Universal Studios
1000 Universal Studios Plaza, Orlando, 32819; tel: 407-363-8000

SPACE COAST
Titusville Area Chamber of Commerce
2000 South Washington Avenue, Titusville, 32780; tel: 321-267-3036; www.titusville.org
Cocoa Beach Area Chamber of Commerce
400 Fortenberry Road, Merritt Island, 32952; tel: 321-459-2200
Melbourne Chamber of Commerce
1005 East Strawbridge Avenue, Melbourne 32901; tel: 321-724-5400

Palm Bay Area Chamber of Commerce
1153 Malabar Road Northeast, Palm Bay; tel: 321-951 9998

Useful Numbers

Police, ambulance or fire service: 911
Local directory inquiries: 411
International directory inquiries: 00
Local operator: 0
International operator: 00
International direct-dial calls: dial 011 + the code of the country, followed by the area or city code minus the first 0. Some country codes:
Australia: 61
Germany: 49
Ireland: 353
New Zealand: 64
United Kingdom: 44

Wheelchairs and Electric Scooters

All theme parks make special considerations for guests requiring the use of wheelchairs or electric scooters. Some rides allow them to be strapped securely in place, whereas assistants at other rides are happy to help transfer guests from their wheelchair to any ride, even the most terrifying roller coasters. The wheelchairs are then moved to the ride's exit and assistants will again help the guest back into the chair – unless, of course, they want to ride again.

Below: tourist information is easy to find.

Food and Drink

It is unfortunate that for most tourists Orlando's food memories are more likely to be a muddled medley of themed restaurants than a cornucopia of subtropical delights. After all, Florida is one of America's most important agricultural states and should be proud of its citrus industry – one of the world's finest. There are also cattle farms and two bodies of fish-filled water providing local produce. Still, you're more likely to be proudly offered Alaskan King Crab than any fresh Floridian fish by your waiter. But if you explore farmers' markets and choose more independent restaurants, you may just find a budding Floridian cuisine.

A Bountiful Harvest

Florida is a major producer of beef, fish, shellfish, and vegetables, and is a world leader in growing citrus fruit. Fierce competition means you'll usually get good value for your money, especially in the type of food America does well: steaks, barbecues, and anything fried.

In the past, theme parks were accused of dishing up only fast food laced with fat and sugar. Now, in response to the adverse publicity, the choice is more varied. The old faithfuls are still available, but the overall style is more

healthy, with plenty of salads, fresh fruit, and frozen yogurt as well as ice cream. Buffets and full-service restaurants in the theme parks and hotels cater to mainstream tastes but have become more adventurous. And, especially in Disney territory, the decor and theming are half the fun.

The problem for most foodies visiting Orlando from abroad will be the lack of fresh produce. Though oranges are usually delicious when in season, there is no emphasis on locally produced fruit and vegetables at the supermarkets. For most Americans if it's

grown in the US, it is local, but the food miles involved in eating a Washington apple in Florida means that your fruit can often be pulpy and tasteless – no wonder processed foods with additives to enhance flavor play such a key part in America's diet.

We list a few farmers' markets below, but for a city of this size they are depressingly thin on the ground.

Farmers' Markets

Celebration
Town Center; Sun 9am–3pm
Fruit and veg stalls open each Sunday, and as this is Disney's hometown there are plenty of arts and crafts activities for kids.

Farmers' Market of Downtown Kissimmee
Toho Square, corner of Darlington and Pleasant Street; Thur 7am–1pm; Link: 4; map p.18
This more functional market offers local produce during the week in Kissimmee's historical downtown setting.

Orlando Farmers' Market
Lake Eola Park; Sun 10am–4pm; Link: 5, 6, 15, 36; map p.135 C2
In addition to fresh produce

Below: Florida produces much of America's fresh fruit and veg.

Left: Florida is known the world over for its citrus crops.

9pm; Link: 39; map p.30

This downstairs deli and wine shop is a gourmand's dream: bread is baked daily, several imported Italian cheeses and sausages are sold, as are fine handmade pastas, sauces, and other Italian extras such as artichokes and sun-dried tomatoes. There is a wide selection of Italian wines and spirits. The coffee is as good as in any café in Italy, and the lunch menu has extensive options, much more than you'd expect from a small café.

Supermarkets

You may find that stocking a villa's cupboards is more of a challenge than you'd expect. Good supermarkets are hard to find, unlike the rundown versions stocking their aisles with Coca-Cola, beer, and pool toys. Below are the details for Orlando's two biggest chains.

Goodings

Lake Buena Vista: SR 535 and I-4; tel: 407-827-1200; www.goodings.com; Link: 300; map p.139 D3

I-Drive: 8255 International Drive; tel: 407-352-4215; I-Ride: mainline; map p.136 A2

Celebration: 29 Blake Boulevard; tel: 321-559-1500; map p.139 C1

Their branches' prime locations near tourist centers make this store a favorite for visitors. They also have an online shopping facility and will deliver to your door for an extra $20.

Publix

www.publix.com

This is a much bigger chain than Goodings, and there are locations all over central Florida. Go to their website to find the one nearest you.

there is gourmet food available from all around the world, and art and craft stalls.

Winter Park Farmers' Market

The old train depot, 200 West New England Avenue; Sat 7am–1pm; Link: 1, 9, 23; map p.135 D4

Considered one of the best farmers' markets in central Florida, its setting in the old train depot adds atmosphere, and there are plenty of fresh baked goods.

G S Produce Market

1111 South Orlando Avenue; tel: 407-623-3377; Mon–Fri 8.30am–7.30pm, Sat until 7pm, Sun 9am–5pm; Link: 39; map p.135 C4

This local farmers' shop is a rare, permanent fresh produce shop. Its business card, which says "next to Krispy Kreme," sums up Orlando's overall attitude to food.

Wine

The Wine Room on Park Avenue

270 Park Avenue South, Winter Park; tel: 407-696-9463; www.thewineroomonline.com; Mon–Wed 10am–10pm, Thur 10am–11pm, Fri and Sat 10am–midnight, Sun noon–7pm; map p.135 D4

A theme park for wine-lovers. There are over 200 wines being served or sold here, and you can taste about 150 of them in quantities as small as 1oz. The cosy leather chairs and well-stocked champagne bar make it worth staying for a while, and there are artisan cheeses and charcuterie to accompany your selections.

Lakeridge Wine Company

19239 US 27 North, Clermont; tel: 352-394-8627; www.lakeridgewinery.com; Mon–Sat 10am–5pm, Sun 11am–5pm

Florida is never going to compete with its west coast rivals for winemaking in the US, but the Lakeridge Wine Company provides an insight into this industry with tours of its production facilities and tastings of its latest vintage. They have won many awards for their wines, especially their whites.

Deli

Antonio's

611 South Orlando Avenue, Maitland; tel: 407-645-1039; www.antoniosonline.com; Mon–Sat 11am–10pm, Sun noon–

Golf

With 150 courses to choose from, you can build an entire vacation around golf in Orlando. Disney World has five championship courses and 15 golf pros. Two courses near Disney, ultramodern Grand Cypress Resort, with a 45-hole course designed by Jack Nicklaus, and Bay Hill Club and Lodge, with its famed Arnold Palmer Golf Academy, are top-rated. Nick Faldo put his stamp on two courses at Marriott's Grand Vista Resort, also on I-Drive. For a complete list of courses, order a copy of the *Golfer's Guide*; tel: 800-864-6101 or go to www.orlandogolfer.com.

Disney Golf

Walt Disney World resort has five championship golf courses, four of which feature regularly on the PGA tour. There are lessons by PGA pros available at all courses, and Disney transportation will take you there, if you are staying on-resort.

Lake Buena Vista

This relatively short course, only 6,749 yards, is a par 73 and set among lighthouses, and enough canals and lakes to create a water hazard for every hole.

Magnolia

Designed by Joe Lee, the course is named after the magnolia trees that surround it and lend the course a unique scent when in blossom. The track is 7,516 yards long.

Oak Trail

This nine-hole course is a bargain compared to other courses at Disney and offers a 50 percent discount on replays. Holes range from 132 to 517 yards, and the design makes it a favorite with developing golfers.

Above: caddie service at Grande Lakes.

Osprey Ridge

Designed by Tom Fazio, this course is 7,101 yards long. The scenery is calmly Floridian, with cypress and bay trees surrounding the course. GPS guidance systems are available, and the clubhouse overlooks a lake and serves food and drink.

Palm

This is one of Disney's most challenging courses. Designed by Joe Lee, the course is surrounded by native Florida woodlands, but

it's the strategically placed palm trees that challenge most golfers. The course is 7,010 yards long.

Golf Resorts

Arnold Palmer's Bay Hill Club and Lodge

9000 Bay Hill Boulevard, Orlando; tel: 888-422-9445; www.bayhill.com

There is so much here other than the golf. Amenities include tennis courts, a spa and salon, a pool, fitness center and restaurants, leaving any golf widows with more than enough to fill their day. The 18-hole course is consistently rated one of the best in Florida by readers of *Golf Digest*. Tuition is provided by the Arnold Palmer Golf Academy.

ChampionsGate Golf Resort

1400 Masters Boulevard, ChampionsGate; tel: 407-787-4653; www.champions gategolf.com

Greg Norman designed these two 18-hole courses attached to the Omni International Hotel. The National course is a traditional

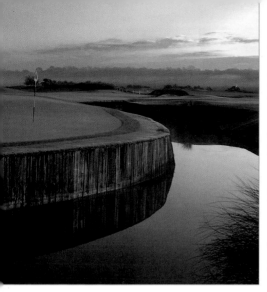

Left: sunrise at Grand Cypress.

World Center Drive, Orlando; tel: 800-380-7931; www.marriottworldcenter.com; map p.139 D2

Just outside the sprawling, convention-oriented Marriott World Center, Hawk's Landing is a favourite with visiting businessmen. The par 71 championsip course is 6,600 yards, and facilities include a pro shop and the Bill Madonna Golf Academy.

Marriott's Grande Vista Resort

5925 Avenida Vista, Orlando; tel: 407-238-7676; http://golf-instruction.marriott-vacations.com; map p.139 E3

Marriott built this resort around the golf. Home to the Nick Faldo Golf Institute, guests arrive here for everything from a three-day to three-hour session. The course is only nine holes, measures 2,300 yards, and is par 32. The unique design challenges golfers to practice and refine a wide variety of shots.

Mystic Dunes Resort and Golf Club

7900 Mystic Dunes Lane, Celebration; tel: 407-787-5678; www.mysticdunesgolf.com

Though not a championship course, Mystic Dunes is just

Orlando has become the capital of Florida's, if not the nation's golf trade. In addition to the 176 golf courses in and around Orlando, the city is also home to the Golf Channel, *Golf Week* magazine, and the site for the annual PGA Merchandise Show. Unsurprisingly, professionals such as Tiger Woods, Arnold Palmer, and Ernie Els call the area home.

the East Nine, added a couple of years later, provides a bit more respite for the less accomplished. The New Course pays homage to St Andrews in Scotland, complete with stone walls and bridges. It is the most challenging of them all. All four courses were designed by Jack Nicklaus.

The Grand Cypress Golf Academy makes the most of these resourceful courses, from short lessons to five day courses.

Hawk's Landing Golf Club

Marriott World Center, 8701

American layout, while the International course recalls the feel of play in Scotland or Ireland.

Grand Cypress Golf Resort

One North Jacaranda, Orlando; tel: 407-239-4700; www.grandcypress.com; map p.139 C4

There are two options available here, the North, South and East Nines or the New Course. The former comprises three nine-hole courses. Golfers combine two of the three to create a full 18-hole round. The original course, a combination of the North and South courses, is very demanding,

Below: morning at Mystic Dunes.

as challenging, but is a bit more capable of accommodating novices, with instruction available and the integration of five sets of tees for golfers of different levels to use. The par 71 course was designed by Gary Koch and stretches 7,012 yards. The Par View GPS system is in use, and there is a 60,000sq-ft clubhouse and a pro shop.

Orange County National Golf Course and Lodge
16301 Phil Ritson Way, Winter Garden; tel: 407-656-2626; www.ocngolf.com

Featuring two 18-hole courses and an award-winning quick nine-hole short course, Orange County makes the most of its natural environment and has yet to be fringed by development – a rarity in any Florida golf course. The prices here are quite steep for a "public" course, and the design and features are not as elite as other area courses.

Orange Lake Resort
8505 West Irlo Bronson Memorial Highway (US 192), Kissimmee; tel: 407-239-0000 or 800-877-6522; www.orange lake.com; map p.138 A2

The Orange Lake resort has four courses: The Legends, designed by Arnold Palmer, and The Reserve are their premier, 18-hole courses with special pricing for resort guests. The nine-hole Legend's Walk, also designed by Arnold Palmer, and Crane's Bend are priced much lower, with more or less equal fees for the public as for the guests.

Orlando hosts two annual PGA tournaments. The Arnold Palmer Invitational in March and the FUNAI Classic in October are both held at the Walt Disney Resort. The LPGA tour visits the Reunion Resort every April for the Ginn open.

Ginn Reunion Resort
1000 Reunion Way, Reunion; tel: 888-418-9610 or 407-662-1000; www.reunionresort.com

The Reunion's three courses have a substantial pedigree: The Legacy, designed by Arnold Palmer, is 6,916 yards and features dramatic elevation changes. The Tradition, designed by Jack Nicklaus, is a more flowing course. The 7,257-yard Independence was designed by Tom Watson, who obviously has a fascination with sand – the last hole is surrounded by 16 bunkers. Also on site is the ANNIKA academy.

Ritz Carlton Golf Club Grande Lakes
4012 Central Florida Parkway, Orlando; tel: 407-206-2400; www.ritzcarlton.com

Two courses are available for guests and the public. The resort's course was designed by Greg Norman, and every golfer is provided with a caddie concierge to assist them on their round. Only five minutes away, Grande Pines is a more challenging course and was designed by Nick Faldo and Steve Smyers. It incorporates the surrounding wetlands into its smart layout.

Rosen Shingle Creek Golf Club
9939 Universal Boulevard, Orlando; tel: 866-996-9933 or 407-996-9933; www.shingle creekgolf.com; map p.136 B1

Shingle Creek meanders through this recently opened course, which does all it can

Below: a bird's-eye view of the Ginn Reunion Resort.

Above: caddies provide expert guidance on how to play their courses.

to incorporate the native flora that existed here before the course's development.

Public Golf Courses

Falcon's Fire Golf Club
3200 Seralago Boulevard, Kissimmee; tel: 407-239-5445; www.falconsfire.com; map p.139 D1

Often cited as one of the best golf courses in Orlando, it is also one of the few not joined to a resort or hotel. The course is well designed, but playable. Even novices are likely to get around without too much frustration. The clubhouse restaurant's menu is available on the golfer's GPS systems, allowing them to deliver food directly to you if you fancy a bite.

MetroWest Golf Club
2100 South Hiawassee Road, Orlando; tel: 407-299-1099; www.metrowestgolf.com

Used as a qualifying course for the Champions Tour and US Open, MetroWest has often been named amongst the best public golf courses in the country. It has teamed up with Universal Studios to offer resort residents special packages. This meticulously maintained course features wide, error-accommodating fairways and spring-fed lakes.

Supplies

Edwin Watts Golf
I-Drive 1: 8330 South International Drive, Orlando; tel: 407-351-1444; www.edwinwatts.com; Mon–Fri 9.30am–8pm, Sat 9.30am–6pm, Sun 11am–5pm; map p.136 A2
I-Drive 2: 7024 International Drive, Orlando; tel: 407-352-2535; Mon–Fri 9.30am–8pm, Sat 9.30am–6pm, Sun 11am–5pm; map p.136 A2
Kissimmee: 2956 Vineland Road; tel: 407-397-4600; map p.139 E1
Airport: 7149 North Frontage Road, Orlando; tel: 407-812-7080; Mon–Fri 9.30am–7pm, Sat 9.30am–6pm, Sun 11am–5pm
Turkey Lake Road: 7501 Turkey Lake Road, Orlando; tel: 407-345-8451; Mon–Fri 9.30am–8pm, Sat 9.30am–6pm, Sun 11am–5pm; map p.136 A2

With stores stretching over the southeast and Massachusetts, Edwin Watts has five branches in the Orlando area. All of them offer cut-price savings in true "outlet mall" fashion, making it easy to stock up on gear while on your golfing vacation.

Travel Agency

GolfOrlando
483 Montgomery Place, Altamonte Springs; tel: 866-342-4782; www.golforlando.com

Specializing in getting people to the land of the Mouse to play golf is a tricky business, but if your trip here has a single focus, GolfOrlando will be happy to oblige.

Below: hole number 18, a destination in itself.

Historical Highlights

15,000–7500 BC
Paleo-Indian hunters – Florida's first "snowbirds" – flee Ice Age glaciers in the north and begin living on the Florida peninsula.

7500–5000 BC
Archaic hunter-gatherers occupy Florida. Archeologists later uncover the first human burials in North America near Cape Canaveral.

1497–1514
French and Spanish claim discovery of Florida. The peninsula appears on a Spanish map in 1510, and Peter Martyr writes in 1514 of a land near the Bahamas with water of eternal youth. Spanish explorers are shipwrecked off Cape Canaveral. Rescued by Timucuans, they marry into the villages and act as interpreters for later Spanish arrivals.

1513
Ponce de León lands in Cape Canaveral area in search of gold, treasure, and the Fountain of Youth. He claims the territory for Spain, naming it *La Florida* – the Land of Flowers. He is killed in 1521 by an Indian arrow.

MID-1700S
Creek Indians – dubbed Seminoles – and runaway African-American slaves, driven south by American settlers, enter Florida.

1764–83
Britain rules Florida.

1774
Quaker naturalist William Bartram of Philadelphia tours Florida. His account inspires many travelers to come to the region.

1783
Britain returns Florida to Spain.

1818

First Seminole War. Future US President Andrew Jackson campaigns against Indians and African-Americans.

1824
The territorial government creates Mosquito County, a vast area extending from near St Augustine to south of Cape Canaveral and west to Alachua County.

1835
The Second Seminole War begins.

1837
Osceola, a half-English, half-Upper Creek Indian fighting with the Seminoles, is imprisoned after entering an American camp under a flag of truce and dies a martyr in 1838.

1842
The Second Seminole War ends with 3,824 Indians and African-Americans being relocated to Arkansas. The federal government offers land to anyone willing to settle near Fort Gatlin, south of Orlando, and act as a citizen-soldier.

1843
Aaron and Isaac Jernigan migrate from Georgia to settle near Fort Gatlin, naming their settlement Jernigan.

1845
Florida becomes a state, with 57,921 residents. Mosquito County changes its name to Orange County in an effort to lure settlers.

1857
Jernigan is renamed Orlando.

1875
Orlando is incorporated (pop. 85) and becomes the seat of Orange County.

1880

Henry Plant's South Florida Railroad is extended to central Florida, allowing expansion of Orlando's agricultural markets.

1884

Fire destroys most of Orlando's downtown business district.

1887

The first African-American township in the United States, Eatonville, is built north of Orlando.

1891

The African-American writer Zora Neale Hurston is born in Eatonville.

1894–9

Severe frosts kill 95 percent of Orange County's citrus groves.

1903

The first automobile is sold in Orlando; the speed limit is 5 miles per hour.

1910–25

A land boom hits Florida. "Tin can tourists" motor to Florida for the winter.

1929

Mediterranean fruit flies devastate the citrus industry. Bok Tower Gardens in Lake Wales are opened by President Calvin Coolidge. African-American physician W.M. Wells opens the Wells' Built Hotel in Orlando as a lodging for jazz musicians.

1949

Gatorland opens.

1950S

Postwar automobile tourism skyrockets.

1957

The Glenn L. Martin Company of Baltimore relocates to Orlando, starting a population boom.

1964

Walt Disney quietly buys more than 28,000 acres of central Florida farmland.

1965

Disney announces plans to build Walt Disney World in Orlando. Interstate 4 opens.

1966

Walt Disney dies.

1971

The Magic Kingdom opens.

1973

SeaWorld Orlando opens.

1990

Universal Studios opens in Florida.

2001

September 11 attacks depress Florida's tourist industry. The effects have yet to fade.

2003

Space Shuttle *Columbia* explodes on re-entry. All seven astronauts die.

2003

Roy Disney, the family's last representative on the board, resigns over disagreements with CEO Michael Eisner.

2005

Eisner resigns amid controversy, but after making Disney one of the world's leading entertainment companies.

2007

Universal Studios announces plans to build the Wizarding World of Harry Potter, a theme park within their Islands of Adventure theme park.

Live Shows, Parades, and Fireworks

Theme parks offer more than thrill rides They produce some fine and some not-so-fine live productions, from the shortened version of *The Lion King* to the unique water shows at SeaWorld. On top of this, Disney's parks come to a standstill each day for a parade of characters and end most nights with fireworks. Dinner theater shows dominate the entertainment menu outside the parks.

Magic Kingdom

LIVE SHOWS
Dream Along with Mickey
Cinderella's Castle stage; see Times Guide

This new show features Mickey and Minnie, and promises that dreams do come true. The royal couple confront a host of other characters, from cynical Donald Duck to the Wicked Witch. Unlike other shows, this provides no respite for sore feet or hot children, as it is performed outside the castle to a standing crowd, where little shade is available.

PARADES
Disney Dreams Come True Parade
Parade starts at Frontierland, travels through Liberty Square and around the hub in front of Cinderella's Castle, and then down Main Street, U.S.A. before its conclusion in Town Square; afternoons daily, usually 3pm, see Times Guide

The lesser of the Magic Kingdom's two parades *(see SpectroMagic below)* still brings the park to a standstill and is a big hit with younger

Above: Mickey at SpectroMagic.

children who can't get enough of waving at famous characters. Unlike Spectro-Magic, this parade is not worth planning for; in fact, if you have teens this would be the perfect time to take advantage of short waiting times and take a couple of spins on Space Mountain *(see Thrill Rides, p.124)*.

SpectroMagic
Parade starts at the park's entrance, Town Square, and continues down Main Street, U.S.A. around the right of the hub and on to Liberty Square, and then ends at Frontierland; it usually starts at 8pm, see Times Guide for days

The Magic Kingdom's nighttime parade only happens a few nights a week, but it is worth planning for, especially as it is always followed by Wishes, the park's fireworks show *(see below)*. In addition to standard-issue characters and music, this show employs spectacular lighting technology on the floats – the Magic Kingdom is even plunged into darkness to heighten its effects. If you are planning to see Wishes afterwards, try to claim a patch on the right side of the hub facing Cinderella's Castle before the parade starts: this will provide excellent viewing for both the parade and the fireworks without you needing to navigate the crowds again.

FIREWORKS
Wishes
Fireworks display is behind Cinderella's Castle; most evenings at closing time, see Times Guide

This is one of the most spectacular fireworks displays you will ever see, and the choreography of live action, music,

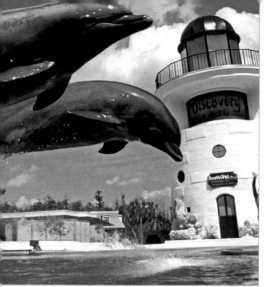

Left: amazing animal tricks at SeaWorld.

see Times Guide

The park's finest show and a great place to cool off. The Festival features animatronic characters from *The Lion King* film as a backdrop, but the main attractions are the performers who include dozens of costumed dancers, singers, gymnasts, ballet dancers, and a fire-eater. The music and per-formances are based on African culture and are of the highest caliber.

Finding Nemo – The Musical

DinoLand U.S.A.; see Times Guide

This is the Animal Kingdom's newest production and it's poor, poor, poor. The overly emotive script condenses the killing, and there is hardly a scene that is free from fishy slaughter. The technique of using live actors carrying

and explosions is faultless – even Disney cynics are likely to be converted by its finale. To get the full effect you must have a clear view of the front of Cinderella's Castle. This makes the hub and the Plaza Restaurant very popular as showtime approaches.

Epcot

IllumiNations: Reflections on Earth

Showcase Lagoon; most evenings at closing time, see Times Guide

The centerpiece of this pyrotechnic spectacular is an enormous Earth globe cre-ated from round LED screens, which hover over the lagoon. Though visible from any-where in World Showcase (Future World is usually closed prior to the perform-ance), the best viewing area is in the Showcase Plaza – the small promontory of land separating Epcot's two lands. The show itself feels a bit long at 15 minutes, much of

which consists of no more than a soundtrack playing as the globe slowly rotates.

Animal Kingdom

LIVE SHOWS

Festival of the Lion King

Camp Minnie Mickey;

Right: Disney's fireworks displays are likely to be the best you've ever seen.

Above: Cirque du Soleil at Downtown Disney.

puppets is also confusing, and at times this seems more of a college theater workshop than the highly accomplished production that is the norm for Disney.

Flights of Wonder
Asia; see Times Guide

This show brings together several exotic bird species to show off their skills, from hunting and diving to uncanny comic timing.

Pocahontas and Her Forest Friends
Camp Minnie Mickey; see Times Guide

There is not much to recommend this short show. The animals make fleeting appearances, and the heavy conservation theme is difficult to take seriously while sitting at a theme park that has overdeveloped acres of Florida's ecosystem. You'd be a fool to stand in line for this.

PARADES
Mickey's Jammin' Jungle Parade
Parade begins in Africa, makes a loop around Discovery Island to Asia and then ends in Africa; daily, see Times Guide

This parade features all the usual characters kitted out in their jungle and safari gear. Dancers from *The Lion King* also make a special appearance.

Hollywood Studios

LIVE SHOWS
Beauty and the Beast – Live on Stage
Sunset Boulevard; see Times Guide

This condensed version of the Disney film is a big hit with children. It lacks the wow factor and air conditioning of other live shows, but often fills up prior to showtimes.

Indiana Jones Epic Stunt Spectacular
Echo Lake; see Times Guide

This 30-minute live show re-creates some of the famous scenes from the Indiana Jones movies. This stunt show is much more accessible and humorous than Lights, Motors, Action! and is a bit less noisy.

Lights, Motors, Action! Extreme Stunt Show
Streets of America; daily, see Times Guide

This must be the loudest show in Orlando! Who'd have thought that such teeny tiny cars could be made to make such an enormous amount of racket. Of course, fans of cars spinning around and making noise will love this type of thing, but for anyone else, this show is a complete waste of time. The Indiana Jones stunt show is much better.

Playhouse Disney – Live on Stage
Animation Courtyard; see Times Guide

Playhouse Disney, the popular children's show, forms the basis for this live production. Its various characters lead young guests through songs and dances.

Voyage of the Little Mermaid
Animation Courtyard; see Times Guide

Though this is one of Disney's more modest live productions, its standards are high, and its intimate setting makes for a great break from outside.

FIREWORKS
Fantasmic!
Sunset Boulevard; see Times Guide, the show is not nightly

During peak seasons, this show fills up fast – it starts seating 90 minutes before the show begins for a reason. Unlike other parks' fireworks shows, it is difficult to appreciate Fantasmic! if you are not in the stadium. The extensive use of lasers and waters to create special effects, not to mention the wide array of live characters, make this almost as much of a Broadway production as a fireworks show. It's well worth the wait to attend.

Downtown Disney

Cirque Du Soleil's La Nouba
West Side; tel: 407-939-1298; www.cirquedusoleil.com; shows Tue–Sat 6 and 9 pm; admission charge

This is the globally acclaimed Cirque's only show in Orlando, and its themes are toned down so that children, too, can appreciate the phenomenal skill of its performers.

Universal Studios

Blue Man Group
CityWalk; tel: 407-224-3200; www.bluemangroup.com; see website or phone for show times; admission charge

The divisive Blue Man Group is not everyone's cup of tea, but their unique blend of mime, dance, music, and technological whiz-bang makes for an interesting evening.

Islands of Adventure

The Eighth Voyage of Sindbad Stunt Show
The Lost Continent; only 2–3 shows daily, see park map for information

Sindbad's efforts to save the princess Amoura never inspire. Though the cave-like set is a perfect backdrop for a drama, the poor acting and tired script lets this production down. Still, no one comes to the Lost Continent to see shows, but to ride thrill rides, and this quixotic show may be just the answer after the shake-up of nearby Dueling Dragons.

Holy Land Experience

Behold the Lamb, Passion Drama
Holy Land Experience *(see p.120)*; shows daily, see park map for information

Disney would never do this to Mickey. The crucifixion of Christ is the key biblical recreation at this park. Though other shows are frequently performed, this is a daily occurrence and the Holy Land's longest-running spectacle. Some people, even those who come to the Holy Land Experience to learn more about their faith, may find they have problems with this production. While it may represent Jesus's sacrifice, it could be criticized for placing him alongside Santa Claus or Peter Pan by recreating it in a theme-park setting. Even if you've no problem with this, remember that the Roman soldiers who are beating the Christ actor and nailing him to a cross may also cause fear and confusion in small children.

SeaWorld

Believe
Shamu Stadium; see show times on park map

For many, this show is the reason they visit SeaWorld. Shamu (a fictional persona for the star whale) has served as SeaWorld's Mickey Mouse since its early days. Though the show and beast are exquisite, the recent revamp has lost its spirit and, compared to viewings a couple of years ago, it seems obvious that Shamu is not just losing steam but also having problems with his dorsal and tail fins as a result of his long confinement. His jumping has suffered, and a sappy storyline displayed on LED screens has tried to take up the slack, but much like the overly patriotic beginning, it attempts to load the audience with emotions rather than educate them about these fascinating creatures.

Blue Horizons
Whale and Dolphin Theater; see show times on park map

This show is a new addition. Previously the Whale and Dolphin Theater featured a

Right: Blue Horizons at the Whale and Dolphin Stadium.

79

Above: Shamu stops for a chat.

fantastic show that showcased the incredible jumping ability of not just dolphins but some smaller whale species, too, while informing the audience about the critters they were admiring. Any such educational aspects have given way to human acrobats who perform for longer than the mammals you've all come to see. The dolphins' repertoire has been seriously cut as well, with the main focus on pretending to be jet skis for the trainers. The show is still an entertaining spectacle that only SeaWorld could accomplish, but its change of focus from education to acrobatics is a real disappointment.

Clyde and Seamore Take Pirate Island
Sea Lion and Otter Stadium; see show times on park map
In front of Pacific Point Preserve is the Sea Lion and Otter Stadium, home to the ridiculously goofy Clyde and Seamore Take Pirate Island show. Scripting a comedy routine around the unpredictable behavior of sea lions, otters, and a giant walrus is foolhardy at best and humiliating to the animals at worst, but the human players incorporate the goofs into the 30-minute show and you'll

laugh in spite of yourself. The pirate ship set is one of the park's best, and it's remarkable to see the animals sliding around the stage and into the tank in front as if Laurel or Hardy were their second names.

Odyssea
Nautilus Theater; see show times on park map
This Cirque du Soleil-style show plays on underwater themes, and the graceful acrobats are as mesmerizing as any fish could wish. Do make this show a priority: you won't be disappointed.

Pets Ahoy
Seaport Theater; see show times on park map
This endearing animal show features cats, dogs, pigs, and other animals rescued from shelters and trained to do remarkable tricks – and shtick. Kids love meeting the actors after the show.

Dinner Shows

Arabian Nights
3081 Arabian Nights Boulevard, Kissimmee; tel: 407-239-9223 or 800-553-6116; www.arabian-nights.com; call for show times; admission charge; Link: 55, 56; map p.139 C1
The most enchanting dinner show in Orlando is Arabian Nights, which stars 50 Ara-

bian, Lippizaner, palomino, and quarter horses that are put through their paces by skilled riders in an enormous arena. The storyline involves the wedding of a prince and princess. The finale is worth the price of admission, featuring 15 riderless horses that prance around the arena as artificial snow falls. Dinner fare includes a choice of chicken tenders, prime rib, or lasagne.

Capone's Dinner and Show
4740 West Irlo Bronson Memorial Highway (US 192), Kissimmee; tel: 407-397-2378 or 800-220-8428; www.alcapones.com; admission charge; Link: 55; map p.18
The longest-running (and weakest) of Orlando's dinner show offerings is the amateurish Capone's. Set in a cheesy 1930s speakeasy

behind a fake ice cream parlor, *Guys and Dolls* this ain't, though the waiters are dressed as gun-brandishing gangsters, and you are ostensibly attending a celebration for the notorious hoodlum Al Capone. Cafeteria-style Italian fare such as lasagne, ziti, spaghetti, and baked chicken is the bill of fare.

Dolly Parton's Dixie Stampede
82511 Vineland Avenue, Orlando; tel: 866-443-4943; www.dixiestampede.com; shows daily, call for times; admission charge; Link: 50, 301–5; map p.139 D3

Guests are divided between Union and Confederates (still a dangerous game to play in some southern states), and the rivalry begins. Over 30 horses dance and prance while you are served a four-course meal, and the stampede includes American buffalo. Despite its name, Dolly Parton does not appear, but patriotic fervor is definitely in attendance.

Medieval Times Dinner and Tournament
4510 West Irlo Bronson Highway (US 192), Kissimmee; tel: 888-WE-JOUST; call for show times; admission charge; Link: 55; map p.18

Medieval Times Dinner is another horsey extravaganza, this one set in the 11th century. It features a well-executed jousting

tournament that pits six knights against each other while the audience cheers on their favorites. Avoid purchasing an upgrade to preferred seating; there are only five rows in the arena, and all offer good viewing.

The Outta Control Magic Comedy Dinner Show
9067 International Drive, Orlando; tel: 407-351-8800; www.wonderworksonline.com; nightly at 6 and 8pm; admission charge; I-Ride: mainline; map p.136 A1

One of the newest entries to the dinner theater scene. Food includes hand-tossed pizza and popcorn with unlimited beer, wine, and soda. Entertainment is a mixture of comedy, improv, and magic that precisely promises to "tickle your funny bone every eight seconds."

Pirate's Dinner Adventure
6400 Carrier Drive, Orlando; tel: 407-248-0590; www.pirates dinneradventure.com; shows nightly, call for times; admission charge; map p.136 A2

A swashbuckling theme prevails at this arena dinner show that has one of Orlando's most impressive sets: a life-size pirate ship

that serves as the centerpiece for an action-packed evening of pillaging, fighting on deck, and attempts to save Princess Anita. Expect to do plenty of oohing and aahing, cheering, and singing of pirate songs. Pre-show attractions include gypsy fortune-tellers and face painting. A post-show Buccaneer Bash continues the silliness.

Sleuth's Mystery Dinner Show
8267 International Drive, Orlando; tel: 407-363-1985 or 800-393-1985; www.sleuths.com; shows change daily, call for times and program; I-Ride: mainline; admission charge; map p.136 A2

This ever-popular dinner theater has recently moved to house more guests. Sleuth's involves the audience in solving a crime and is perfect for fans of murder mystery weekends and whodunits. Guests are seated at round tables to watch the first act, which gets the murdering over with and includes much ad lib at the audience's expense. Each table then chooses a spokesperson who questions the actors as you try to solve the murder.

Below: some wonder why Dolly Parton's Dixieland Stampede has yet to buy into the current fashion for overt patriotism.

If Sleuth's has whetted your appetite for murder, there's a competitor in town. The concept is similar, but the food is much better at the **Murder-watch Mystery Theater** in the Grosvenor Resort Hotel *(see Accommodations, p.41)*; unfortunately, the show plays only on Saturday night.

Museums and Galleries

D ue to its relative youth and its inherent associaton with theme parks, Orlando's cultural legacy is often overlooked. While it may never compete with the likes of New York or Chicago in terms of museum space, it has several fascinating institutions that record its unique roles in southern American history. Its climate has offered a welcome home to acclaimed artists in their latter years, and there are state-of-the-art museums such as the Orlando Science Center. All of these make for a great, real-world day out.

History

The Historic Waterhouse Residence and Carpentry Shop Museums
820 Lake Lily Drive, Maitland; tel: 407-644-2451; Thur–Sun noon–4pm; admission charge; Link: 1, 9; map p.30

When William H. Waterhouse settled in Maitland at the end of the 19th century, he was a pioneer. By the time he'd completed his home here, he had become one of the area's most in-demand builders. This house has been fully restored to show how he and

his family would have lived on the shores of Lake Lily. Waterhouse built this house himself using basic tools like those found in the Carpentry Shop Museum. Staff hold demonstrations and workshops that let you try the tools out for yourself. The house is viewed by tour only, but the tour guide is a very enjoyable chap who brings the house and the community alive with his insight. There is also a self-guided tour through a traditional Victorian herb garden.

Below: the Historic Waterhouse Residence.

Holocaust Memorial Resource and Education Center
815 North Maitland Avenue, Maitland; tel: 407-628-0555; Mon–Thur 9am–4pm, Fri 9am–1pm, Sun 1–4pm; admission charge; map p.30

A somber experience awaits visitors here. One room chronicles the history of the Holocaust with multimedia displays. Another room offers changing exhibits on aspects

After the building of Henry Plant's and Henry Flagler's railroad networks in the 1880s and 1890s, central Florida was carved open to greater visitation and settlement, and towns like Winter Park and Maitland sprang up beside the tracks. Upper-class Englishmen, attracted by the idea of being plantation owners and enjoying an easy outdoor lifestyle far from home, rushed to purchase land from state and railway corporations at a dollar an acre. The new land also lured working-class Englishmen hoping to escape the strictures of home.

Left: the Orlando Science Center.

Winter Park Telephone Company, which was founded in 1910 to improve the custom at a local grocery.

Orange County Regional History Center
65 East Central Boulevard, Orlando; tel: 407-836-8500; www.thehistorycenter.org; Mon–Sat 10am–5pm, Sun noon–5pm; admission charge; Link: 3, 6, 7, 11, 13, 18, 51; map p.135 C2

OCRHC now occupies the restored 1927 Orange County Courthouse in Downtown's Heritage Square, the old Orlando town center. The museum, now an affiliate of the Smithsonian Institution, features four floors of colorful exhibits covering central Florida's 12,000 years of history, from the state's first Indian residents to Spanish explorers and missionaries, British colonists, the Seminole Indian Wars, Cracker cowmen, citrus-growers, tin can tourists, aerospace engineers, and Walt Disney.

of the Nazi campaign to exterminate Jews, homosexuals, gypsies, and other minorities. A library holds 4,000 volumes dedicated exclusively to Holocaust history. Special events include a Kristallnacht Commemoration in November.

Maitland Historical Museum and Telephone Museum
221 West Packwood Avenue, Maitland; tel: 407-644-1364; Thur–Sun noon–4pm; admission charge; Link: 39; map p.30

The Maitland Historical Museum displays old pictures, artifacts, and other items that tell the story of Maitland's development from the pioneer days to the development of lumber and citrus industries. The Telephone Museum has a collection of early phones from the

Below: Bunk Baxter was famed for his alligator-wrestling ability.

Above: so many ways to be eaten alive at the Orlando Science Center.

The area's little-known Indian cultures are particularly well interpreted, with dioramas showing an ancient shell midden, Timucuan chiefs in ceremonial attire, 3,000-year-old St John's pottery (probably among the first to be made in North America), and contemporary Seminole culture, including a video of the Green Corn Ceremony held annually by the few hundred Seminoles still living in the Everglades.

A community museum in the best sense, OCRHC offers monthly socials and educational programs for people of all ages. Some of the best are for children. Camp-ins give them the opportunity to sleep overnight among the exhibits. Other school programs allow kids to perform mock trials of the Big Bad Wolf and other fairy-tale characters in the original courtroom where, less innocently, mass murderer Ted Bundy was tried and sentenced to death.

Wells' Built Museum
511 West South Street, Orlando; tel: 407-245-7535; www.pastinc.org; Mon–Fri 9am–5pm; admission charge; Link: 39; map p.134 C2
This museum has the best story of any cultural institution in Orlando. Set in the old Wells' Built Hotel, this was the center of African American culture in Orlando from 1926 until the end of segregation. It housed legends from every walk of life, including Ella Fitzgerald, Thurgood Marshall, and Jackie Robinson. A casino nightclub stood next door at the time and hosted such big-name acts as Ray Charles and B.B. King.

It's no exaggeration to say that the history of this building holds more significance to the recent cultural history of the United States than all the other museums in this book combined. It is a great pity that the city and state authorities don't provide the money the museum so obviously needs to continue to improve its facilities.

Science

Orlando Science Center
777 East Princeton Street, Loch Haven Park, Orlando; tel: 407-514-2188; www.osc.org; museum Sun–Thur 10am–6pm, Fri–Sat 10am–9pm, observatory Fri 6–9pm, Sat 6–9pm; admission charge; map p.135 C3
Ten interactive exhibit halls cover everything from Florida's famous limestone sinkholes to its dinosaurs (courtesy of Disney World), an astronaut's life in zero gravity, and a journey through the human body. An eight-story CineDome shows giant-

Below: the Crosby Observatory at the Science Center.

screen films, and daily sky shows are presented in the Planetarium, including one on Orlando's night sky, which can be viewed through a giant telescope in the Crosby Observatory.

Art

Albin Polasek Museum and Sculpture Gardens
633 Osceola Avenue, Winter Park; tel: 407-647-6294; www.polasek.org; Tue–Sat 10am–4pm, Sun 1am–4pm; admission charge; Link: 23; map p.30

Listed in the National Register of Historic Places, the home of late Czech-American sculptor Albin Polasek is a peaceful 3-acre retreat with a studio, private chapel, gardens, and galleries. The collection of some 200 pieces are dominated by Polasek's works, many of them artfully displayed on the manicured grounds. The museum also exhibits sculpture by American masters such as Augustus Saint-Gaudens.

Charles Hosmer Morse Museum of American Art
445 North Park Avenue, Winter Park; tel: 407-645-5311; www.morsemuseum.org; admission charge; map p.135 D4

Featuring the world's most comprehensive collection of

Above: the Charles Hosmer Morse Museum.

late-19th-century stained glass by Louis Comfort Tiffany, the centerpiece of the collection is the reconstructed Tiffany Chapel, designed for the 1893 World's Columbian Exposition in Chicago. The museum was founded in 1942 by Jeannette Genius McKean and named for her industrialist grandfather, a Winter Park benefactor. The collections were assembled over 50 years by Mrs McKean and her husband Hugh McKean, president of Rollins College in Winter Park, and include significant holdings of Arts and Crafts-style Rookwood pottery and American painting.

Cityartsfactory
29 South Orange Avenue, Orlando; tel: 407-648-7060; www.cityartsfactory.com;

gallery hours vary; free; Link: 3, 6, 7, 11, 13, 18, 51; map p.135 C2

Set in the recently renovated Philips Theater building, the Cityartsfactory hosts five art galleries which include African art, glassworks, and other contemporary works. The upstairs performance space has a good view of the city and is open for scheduled events only.

Cornell Fine Arts Museum
Rollins College, 1000 Holt Avenue, Winter Park; tel: 407-646-2526; www.rollins.edu/cfam; Tue–Sat 10am–5pm, Sun 1–5pm; admission charge; Link: 23; map p.135 D4

Though quite small, the Cornell Museum of Fine Arts, on the gracious Mediterranean-style campus of Rollins College, is one of the finest and oldest art museums in the

Below: fine examples of Morse's work with the Tiffany Chapel in the middle.

southeast. Each year, the Cornell stages six to eight exhibitions drawn from its holdings of more than 6,000 European and American works of art. The collection encompasses paintings, drawings, and sculpture from the 1450s to the 1990s. At the start of the school year, one gallery is dedicated to exhibiting work by contemporary local artists.

Grand Bohemian Gallery
Grand Bohemian Hotel, 325 South Orange Avenue, Orlando; tel: 407-581-4801; www.grand

bohemiangallery.com; Link: 3, 6, 7, 11, 13, 18, 51; map p.135 C2
Set on the ground floor of the Grand Bohemian Hotel, there's no problem attracting moneyed clients into this cramped but intriguing gallery, which is possibly one of Orlando's finest commercial galleries for contemporary American and European fine art. The collection is constantly changing, with new imports replacing purchased pieces and special exhibitions featuring single artists occurring throughout the year.

Maitland Art Center
231 West Packwood Avenue, Maitland; tel: 407-539-2181; Mon–Fri 9am–4.30pm, Sat and Sun noon–4.30pm; www.maitlandartcenter.org; free; Link: 39; map p.30
Tranquil grounds and artworks are the features of this sprawling, 6-acre art studio complex on a quiet side street. It was built in the 1930s by artist Jules Andre Smith. A formed concrete building decorated with an unusual Aztec-Mayan frieze, it is considered one of the best surviving examples of fantasy architecture. Smith, a friend of Annie Russell, the New York actress who was professor of Theater Arts at Rollins College *(see Annie Russell Theatre, p.89)*, moved to Maitland in the early 1930s and designed sets for productions at the quaint Annie Russell Theatre. In 1937, a donation from the wife of Edward Bok, the Dutch-born former editor of *Ladies' Home Journal*, allowed Smith to build a "laboratory studio

Below: the Aztec-inspired building of the Maitland Art Center.

to be devoted to research in modern art." Now managed by the Maitland Historical Society, the little museum's galleries and grounds (reputed to be haunted by Smith's ghost) still retain an aging charm. Changing exhibitions are devoted to art representing many different ethnic traditions within the community.

Menello Museum of American Art
900 East Princeton Street, Loch Haven Park, Orlando; tel: 407-246-4278; www.mennello museum.org; Tue–Sat 10.30am–4.30pm; Sun noon–4.30pm; admission charge; map p.135 C3
One of only a handful of American folk art museums, much of the Menello's collection is devoted to the colorful paintings of Earl Cunningham, a self-taught artist and former sea captain whose long friendship with the Menellos led to the founding of this museum. Special exhibitions of American folk art are always on display as well.

Left: a painting by Earl Cunningham.

Millenia Fine Art Gallery
555 South Lake Destiny Drive, Orlando; tel: 407-304-8100 or 866-655-8655; www.millenia fineart.com; Mon–Fri 9am–5pm; free; Link: 24, 40, 305; map p.136 B3
This 30,000sq-ft gallery is part of the Millenia art chain that exhibits contemporary art for sale across the country. The artists on their roster include Dale Chihuly, Henry Moore, and Marc Chagall, among others. Artists change regularly.

Orlando Museum of Art
2416 North Mills Avenue, Loch Haven Park, Orlando; tel: 407-896-4231; www.omart.org; Tue–Sat 10am–5pm, Sun noon–5pm; admission charge; map p.135 C3
Founded in 1924 and recently expanded, OMA's well-regarded collections include ancient artifacts from the American southwest, Mexico, and Central and South America, works by 18th- to 20th-century American painters such as John Singer Sargent, Thomas Moran, Georgia O'Keeffe, and Robert Rauschenberg, and African art. The museum also hosts temporary exhibitions, which tend to focus on art of the Americas.

Zora Neale Hurston National Museum of Fine Arts
227 East Kennedy Boulevard, Eatonville; tel: 407-647-3131; www.zoranealehurston.cc; Mon–Fri 9am–4pm; donations suggested; Link: 1, 9; map p.30
Devoted to African-American culture, this tiny museum in Eatonville, the first black township in the United States, is named for Hurston, the noted Harlem Renaissance writer, anthropologist, and folklorist, who was born in Eatonville in 1891. She celebrated rural Florida life in such books as *Their Eyes Were Watching God* and *Of Men and Mules*. Revolving exhibitions feature African-American art. Each January, Eatonville holds a festival in Hurston's honor.

Below: Zora Neale Hurston and a Chiuly exhibit at the Orlando Museum of Art.

Music, Dance, and Theater

Suffering the same fate as Orlando's museums, the performing arts outside of the theme parks are too often ignored by visitors. What a shame. The Annie Russell Theatre is one of the longest established theaters in the state: set on the lovely campus of Rollins College, it has a wide range of productions. The accomplished Shakespeare Theater and eccentric Mad Cow round off the drama. Orlando maintains professional opera, philharmonic, and ballet companies, which perform mostly at the Bob Carr Performing Arts Center.

Music

CLASSICAL

MUSIC COMPANIES

Orlando Opera
1111 North Orange Avenue, Orlando; tel: 407-426-1700; www.orlandoopera.org
The season runs from October to April and includes grand productions such as Mozart's *Don Giovanni* and *Turandot* by Puccini. Performances are at the Bob Carr Performing Arts Center.

Orlando Philharmonic
812 East Rollins Street, Suite 300, Orlando; tel: 407-770-0071; www.orlandophil.org
Established in the early 1990s, the Orlando Phil has yet to find a permanent home, instead performing at two regular venues. Its main series is Phil at Carr, which focuses on classical music performed at the Bob Carr Performing Arts Center. It also runs a family series at this venue that features more child-oriented works like *Peter and the Wolf*. The company performs smaller classical productions at the Orlando Shakespeare Theater.

VENUES

Bob Carr Performing Arts Center
401 Livingston Street, Orlando; tel: 407-839-3900; www.orlandovenues.net; Link: 8; map p.134 C2
A year-round community auditorium that hosts regional and national musical, theater, and dance performances.

JAZZ

CityJazz
CityWalk; map p.50
The only place for jazz in the theme parks. Styles range from Chicago blues to bebop. The menu features light fare and about 60 wines, or simply choose a drink from the rolling martini cart. More than 500 objects are on display here in *Downbeat* magazine's Jazz Hall of Fame.

Dance

Central Florida Ballet
4525 Vineland Road, Suite 204, Orlando; tel: 407-849-9948;

Right: CityJazz is the only music venue in the theme parks offering more than DJs.

Left: the accomplished Orlando Shakespeare Theater.

productions suitable for a younger audience and the entire family by transferring classic fairy tales and children's books to the stage. Weekend matinees are especially popular.

Annie Russell Theatre
Rollins College, 1000 Holt Avenue, Winter Park; tel: 407-646-2145; www.rollins.edu/theatre; map p.135 D4
Seating over 300, the Annie is no simple college theater. It is at the heart of the oldest theater program in Florida and has a reputation as one of the most prestigious small theaters in America. Its program is eclectic and includes everything from rep plays by Oscar Wilde to improv, new material, and murder mystery productions. It also hosts the Rollins Dance series.

www.centralfloridaballet.com; map p.136 B4
This academy for dance holds a few productions each year in its intimate Studio Theater. Its *Nutcracker* is a bit of a Christmas tradition. Other shows include the original *9/11 An American Moment* as well as traditional favorites.

Orlando Ballet
1111 North Orange Avenue; tel: 407-426-1733; www.orlandoballet.org; map p.135 D4
Central Florida's only fully professional ballet company, its season runs from October to May and includes a Christmas *Nutcracker* as well as other light-hearted productions such as *The Pirates of Penzance*. Performances are all at the Bob Carr Performing Arts Center.

Theater

Mad Cow Theater
105 South Magnolia Avenue, Orlando; tel: 407-297-8788; www.madcowtheater.com; map p.135 C2
Just over 10 years old, the Mad Cow has established itself as a key player in the

Downtown arts scene. The work provides a platform for up-and-coming American talent while staging established theater from around the world and occasional rep pieces.

Orlando Shakespeare Theater
812 East Rollins Street, Loch Haven Park, Orlando; tel: 407-447-1700; www.orlandoshakes.org; map p.135 C3
The Orlando Shakespeare Theater began nearly 20 years ago as a month-long festival and has since grown into a year-round theater; it is now partnered by the University of Central Florida, which provides further educational resources. Of course, the season is dominated by the Bard's works, but there is room for modern playwrights, too, especially those with a strong literary streak.

The Rep
1001 East Princeton Street, Loch Haven Park, Orlando; tel: 407-896-7365; www.orlandorep.com; map p.135 C3
The Rep pays special attention to providing affordable

Several seasonal productions add variety to Orlando's cultural scene. Winter Park's **Bach Festival** (www.bachfestivalflorida.org), in February and March, highlights the region's talents in classical music. **Broadway Across America** (www.broadwayacrossamerica.com) brings first-rate touring productions to the Bob Carr Performing Arts Center. The **Festival of Orchestras** (www.festivaloforchestras.com) brings acclaimed international orchestras from as far away as Russia to Orlando for a series of concerts each winter. In May, the **Orlando International Fringe Festival** brings over 500 performances of theater, music and comedy to Downtown Orlando for 10 days. It's the oldest non-juried fringe festival in the United States.

Natural World

When Juan Ponce de León landed at Cape Canaveral in 1513, he found a unique blend of savagery and beauty. What would later become Florida was already populated by over 150,000 peoples who were creating some of the most sophisticated pottery in the Americas at the time. On the other hand, the boggy land gave way under your feet, man-eating alligators inhabited every body of water, and the air was infested with malaria-carrying mosquitoes. Still, he chose the name La Florida (Land of Flowers). The beauty that so impressed him is remarkably well preserved if you know where to look.

Animal Interaction

Green Meadows Petting Farm

1368 South Poinciana Boulevard, Kissimmee; tel: 407-846-0770; www.greenmeadowsfarm.com; daily 9.30am–5pm; admission charge; map p.18

It wasn't long ago that this area supplied cattle that made Kissimmee the center of the ranching industry in Florida. The animals are here now more to provide fun and education for local children. Train rides and traditional hay rides are also available, and guests are welcome to milk the cows.

Parks and Gardens

Audubon Center for Birds of Prey

1101 Audubon Way, Maitland; tel: 407-644-0190; www.audubonflorida.org; daily 10am–4pm; admission charge; map p.30

The Birds of Prey Center is hidden in a residential area near Lake Sibelia between Maitland and Eatonville. But don't let this dissuade you. The recently refurbished raptor rescue center offers an unforgettable experience. Audubon takes in about 600 injured birds a year and releases 40 percent of them.

You won't see recuperating birds here – they are isolated to improve their odds of survival in the wild – but you will see members of some 32 raptor species whose injuries are so extensive they can only survive in captivity. Ospreys, tiny screech owls, vultures, bald eagles, red-tailed hawks, kites, and other birds of prey live in aviaries. A program also allows you to adopt a particular bird (they all have names) to help the center with its work. Guided tours for groups of 10 or more are available by reservation.

Canaveral National Seashore

map p.32

Adjacent to the Merritt Island Wildlife Refuge is the 57,000-acre Canaveral National Seashore, whose miles of barrier dunes and sea-swept beaches are a haven for beachcombers and nature-lovers. Two of the beaches, Apollo and Playalinda, at the northern and southern tips of the seashore, have restrooms, boardwalks, and, from May 30 to September 1, lifeguards. In between, the

Below: don't be fooled by the charming smile.

Left: exotic plants dominate the Leu Gardens.

Merritt Island National Wildlife Refuge
map p.32

At the 140,000-acre Merritt Island National Wildlife Refuge, adjacent to Kennedy Space Center, endangered West Indian manatees loll peacefully in brackish lagoons, sea turtles waddle ashore to lay eggs on pristine beaches, and alligators bask in the sun on creek banks. The refuge lies along a prime migratory flyway, and the sky is filled in early spring with warblers and shorebirds while, on the ground, egrets and herons are in breeding plumage, wood storks and ospreys build nests, and bald eaglets test their wings.

The mild climate and varied environment of marshes, hardwood hammocks, pine forest, scrub, and coastal dunes sustain more than 500 species of wildlife, including more than 20 on the Endangered or Threatened Species List. This is one of the most important nesting areas in the country for loggerhead, green, and leatherback turtles.

Much of the wildlife can be spotted along the 7-mile, one-way **Black Point Wildlife Drive**, a self-guided auto tour through salt- and freshwater marshes. The entrance is on SR 406, a mile east of the intersection with SR 402. Manatees, most prevalent in the spring and fall, can be best viewed from the observation area near Haulover Canal Bridge on SR 3.

The best time to visit is during the off-season, when wildlife populations are at their highest, and mosquitoes, high temperatures, and thunderstorms are least likely to present a problem.

Walt Disney World Resort has only ever closed once – when Hurricane Andrew threatened in 1992.

landscape has been left untouched. Portions of the seashore may be closed for days before shuttle launches or when parking lots are full.

Harry P. Leu Gardens
1920 North Forest Avenue, Orlando; tel: 407-246-2620; www.leugardens.org; daily 9am–5pm; admission charge; map p.28

After days at chaotic theme parks, your sanity deserves a break at a quiet retreat like Leu Gardens. The grounds are made for gentle strolls and spending the day. The gardens were founded to inspire visitors to appreciate the plantlife of central Florida and the **Native Wetland Garden** supports a lot of native wildlife and birds, including alligators.

Other tropical environments are recreated here as well as more domestic features such as a rose, vegetable, herb, and butterfly gardens.

In the center of the grounds stands the original **Leu House,** which can be viewed by guided tour only and illustrates what life in Florida was like at the beginning of the 20th century.

If you want to delve a bit deeper into Florida's natural world, the gardens offer regular courses ranging from birdwatching to rose gardening. The gardens also show films on their Date Nights on the first Friday of each month in addition to staging other events.

Below: a hatchling begins its solitary journey.

Nightlife

Orlando's theme parks do an excellent job of keeping their clientele after hours, which is a shame, as Downtown (Orlando's not Disney's) is worth the excursion. Downtown Disney and CityWalk, on the other hand, have restaurants, bars, and clubs all centrally located with transportation back to resort hotels until late evening, so you need not worry about drink-driving. Downtown Orlando is exactly what you'd expect from a modern city: a mixture of stylish clubs and bars, some characterful watering holes, and a large variety of independent restaurants. The choice is yours.

Downtown Disney

Adventurers Club

Pleasure Island; map below
Perhaps the most unusual place in Pleasure Island – part bar, part interactive theater, part Disney imagineering. The concept behind this club is that it is really a dusty old gentlemen's club established by long-lost explorer Merriweather Adam Pleasure. The place is decked out in primitive masks, shrunken heads, archeological relics, and stuffed animals (some of which talk), and staffed with actors who draw guests into improvisational encounters. Be sure to hang around for one of the 20-minute cabaret-comedy shows held in the library, and don't be surprised if you get dragged into the act.

BET SoundStage Club

Pleasure Island; map below
Spread over two floors, this club takes its name from the Black Entertainment Television network. The club plays hip-hop, reggae, and old-school R&B.

8 Trax

Pleasure Island; map below
This retro 70s club desperately tries to breathe new life into dusty disco hits. You're

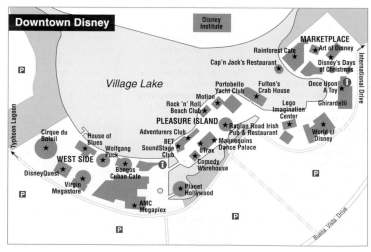

Downtown Disney

Disney Institute

MARKETPLACE

Rainforest Cafe · Art of Disney

Cap'n Jack's Restaurant · Disney's Days of Christmas

Village Lake

Portobello Yacht Club · Fulton's Crab House · Once Upon A Toy

Motion

Rock 'n' Roll Beach Club · Lego Imagination Center · Ghirardelli

PLEASURE ISLAND

Cirque du Soleil · House of Blues · Adventurers Club · Raglan Road Irish Pub & Restaurant · World of Disney

Wolfgang Puck · BET SoundStage Club · Mannequins Dance Palace · 8 Trax

WEST SIDE

DisneyQuest · Bongos Cuban Cafe · Comedy Warehouse

Virgin Megastore · Planet Hollywood

AMC Megaplex

Typhoon Lagoon

International Drive

Buena Vista Drive

Left: Glo Lounge on International Drive.

House of Blues does still attract some fine artists.

COMEDY
Comedy Warehouse
Pleasure Island; map left
This will begin any night at Pleasure Island on an upbeat note. The improvised routines are a hoot, and the comics are experts at working an audience. There are five 45-minute shows a night; the first two are the least crowded.

Disney's Boardwalk
Atlantic Dance Hall
Boardwalk Resort
This mock pier serves as the only nightclub in the Board-walk area. The Art Deco interior plays on further coastal themes, but the crowd (this is Disney) is tame when the DJ attempts to kick it up every night.

CityWalk
Red Coconut Club
Sun–Thur 8pm–2am and Fri–Sat 6pm–2am; map p.50
The Red Coconut sits on CityWalk's upper level, affording a view of the throngs below and the quiet

Below: the taste and sound of the deep south.

All of Pleasure Island's night-clubs are covered by one entrance fee, just over $20. You must have ID to prove you are over 21 years of age to enter most clubs. Underaged guests are alowed at Adventurers Club and Comedy Warehouse, so long as they are accompanied by a person over 21.

unlikely to leave without some fool dancing to *YMCA*, and the falsetto Bee Gees numbers lurk around every corner.
Mannequins Dance Palace
Pleasure Island; map left
Mannequins is Pleasure Island's most extravagant dance club – a multilevel mannequin warehouse (at Disney, everything has a back story) with a revolving dance floor, state-of-the-art laser lights, several bars, and an earthshaking sound system. Disney cast members sometimes come here after hours, and there are occasional outbreaks by professional dancers. Ask at the desk if there's anything scheduled.

Motion
Pleasure Island; map left
A massive video screen projects the latest top 40 videos as pretty young things revel in the deciduous songs of their youth. The crowd is divided between locals and young adults desperate to abandon their older family members after a day at the park.
Rock 'n' Roll Beach Club
Pleasure Island; map left
This three-story beach house tricked out in a surf club motif features top-notch bands bashing out rock classics from the 1960s to today. There's a dance floor on the first level, and bar-room games like air hockey, darts, and billiards on the floors above.

LIVE MUSIC
House of Blues
Westside; tel: 407-934-BLUE; www.hob.com; map left
Though the venue of this chain bar provides little character, and Downtown Disney could not possibly be any further away from the Bayou in terms of attitude, the

93

Above: CityWalk's
newest Club.

lagoon beyond. If you are looking for a bit of peace and quiet, the indoor tables are the best bet; the area around the bar is better suited for those wanting to take in the live music or DJs.

the groove
Sun–Thur 8pm–2am and Fri–Sat 6pm–2am; map p.50
The crowd is mostly young and single at this cavernous dance club equipped with kaleidoscopic lights, a mist machine, and a mind-numbing sound system that pumps out techno, house, and hip-hop. A warren of intimate themed rooms with color-coded drinks is the place for conversation.

Kissimmee and Celebration

Sun on the Beach
Old Town, 5770 West Irlo Bronson Memorial Highway (US 192), Suite 222; tel: 407-397-0207; www.sobafterdark.com; daily 9pm–2am; admission charge; Link: 55; map p.139 D1
If the Old Town shopping center does anything well it's this: raucous nightlife. This is the best nightclub on the US 192 stretch. Entertainment changes nightly, and there is a regular Bike Night, though that might put off leather-phobes.

International Drive and Lake Buena Vista

Destiny Nightclub
7430 Universal Boulevard, Orlando; tel: 407-351-9800; www.destinynightclub.net; Wed–Sat; Link: 21; map p.136 A2
This was one of the first nightclubs to attempt to take on the fickle I-Drive crowd. It's loud, and the floor gets packed, all 23,000sq ft of it, with beautiful people from all over the world. There are even beds, for guests to relax in, of course.

Glo Lounge Orlando
8967 International Drive, Orlando; tel: 407-351-0361; www.goloungeorlando.com; Wed–Fri 6pm–2am, Sat and Sun 9pm–2am; admission charge; I-ride: mainline; map p.136 A1
Glo Lounge has the subtle neon-lit atmosphere of a chill-out lounge, but its identity is not so clear-cut. In addition to various thumping dance evenings, there are billiard tables and large-screen plasma televisions that show sporting events. The result is an ever-changing crowd somewhat less glamorous than their surroundings.

Downtown and Loch Haven Park

Antigua
41 West Church Street, Orlando; tel: 407-649-4270; www.churchstreetbars.com; Tue, Thur–Sun; map p.135 C2
A 20ft cascading waterfall and two 500-gallon fish tanks set the tone in this sleek, seductively lit nightclub. The sound system makes all audio contact impossible, but the multilevel layout makes finding your niche in the night no problem.

Club at Firestone
578 North Orange Avenue, Orlando; tel: 407-872-0066; www.clubatfirestone.com; Thur–Sun; Link: 3, 6, 7, 11, 13, 18, 51; map p.135 C2
The daddy of all Orlando clubs. On the scene now for over 15 years, it has been praised by everyone from MTV to Univision for its promotion of underground music – mostly hip-hop and electronica. An accomplished institution.

Dolce Nightclub
122 West Church Street, Orlando; tel: 407-849-0808; www.dolcenightclub.com; Wed–Sat; map p.135 C2
A strict dress code keeps the riff-raff out of this new club. Originally called Club Paris after Paris Hilton, the heiress has been dropped

Below: several bars in Orlando brag about their signature martinis and margaritas.

Right: Glo features pool tables for those needing distraction from the dance floor.

from her pedestal and a sweeter name has been adopted. The crowd, still full of beautiful starlets, have yet to clock any difference. The exclusive VIP areas come at a price, as does the selection of cocktails.

Roxy Nightclub

740 Bennett Road, Orlando; tel: 407-898-4004; www.roxy orlando.com; Tue–Sun; map p.135 C2

The only problem with the Roxy is that it is tucked away beyond even Thornton Park, with nothing else going on around it. Otherwise it's an accomplished club night every night, with a large dance floor and heavy sound system.

Slingapour's

17 Wall Street Plaza, Orlando; tel: 407-849-9904; www.wall streetplaza.com; Link: 3, 6, 7, 11, 13, 18, 51; map p.135 C2

Located in the busy Wall Street Plaza area, this late-opening club takes in the revelers as they leave the bars and restaurants – expect a few wrinkled suits to appear after a hard day at the office. Happy-hour specials on martinis.

Tabu

46 North Orange Avenue, Orlando; tel: 407-648-8363; www.tabunightclub.com; Tue–Sun; Link: 3, 6, 7, 11, 13, 18, 51; map p.135 C2

Unless you limit yourself to resort nightclubs at CityWalk or Downtown Disney, getting back after a night out is not an easy task. Public transport in the later hours is non-existent. A taxi is your only option, and taking one, even a short distance, is very expensive.

This club doesn't open its doors without getting crammed. It's an oldie on Orlando's scene and has developed a reputation for top DJs and wild nights.

LIVE MUSIC

Independent Bar

70 North Orange Avenue, Orlando; tel: 407-839-0457; www.independentbar.net; Link: 3, 6, 7, 11, 13, 18, 51; map p.135 C2

The main attractions at the Independent Bar are the live acts, but even on a non-concert night it still has two floors of dancing, each with their own music and an outdoor café area to unwind in.

The Social

54 North Orange Avenue, Orlando; tel: 407-246-1419; www.thesocial.org; Link: 3, 6, 7, 11, 13, 18, 51; map p.135 C2

The premier place in the Orlando area to catch live music acts, from indie rock-

ers to electronica. The cavernous club was once the only place in Orlando for touring acts to perform. Now with competition from larger venues at the amusement parks its importance has been reduced, but nothing can destroy its history.

COMEDY

SAK Comedy Lab

380 West Amelia Street, Orlando; tel: 407-648-0001; www.sak.com; Tue–Sat; Link:4, 17, 19; map p.134 C2

The clever improv team at SAK don't just make their audience laugh, they train students to make their audience laugh, too. The key production is performed by the Ensemble, a professional improv team. Less expensive productions are performed by the Lab Rats. As the name suggests, these are students still learning the trade.

95

Pampering

After a hard day at the park you need to put your feet up. After an entire week of it, serious therapy may be needed to restore both body and soul. Though resorts are yet to examine their customers' heads, they have begun to appoint some of the finest spa facilities available in the southeast US. Big-name operators like Canyon Ranch and Mandara Spa have opened local outlets, Disney's Grand Floridian has gone so far as to create its own line of beauty products, and there is no shortage of fine establishments in the larger resort hotels which cater to conventioners and vacationers alike.

Canyon Ranch SpaClub at Gaylord Palms
6000 West Osceola Parkway, Kissimmee; tel: 407-586-2051; www.canyonranch.com; map p.139 C1
This full-service 20,000sq-ft spa offers traditional treatments, plus full nutrition and wellness counseling and fitness training. Its specialty is the Canyon Stone Massage that uses smooth volcanic stones, gently warmed.

Grand Floridian Health Club and Spa
Grand Floridian Resort and Spa, 4401 Grand Floridian Way, Lake Buena Vista; tel: 407-824-2332; www.relaxedyet.com; daily 6am–9pm; map p.138 A4
Run by the Niki Bryan Spa company, this is one of two full-service spas available at Disney World. Set in the lush surrounds of the Grand Floridian Resort, this lavish spa offers complete massage therapies, and special treatments for couples and young children.

Mandara Spa at Portofino
Portofino Bay Hotel, 5601 Universal Boulevard, Orlando; tel:

407-503-1244; www.mandara spa.com; fitness Center 6am–10pm; spa and salon 7am–10pm; map p.136 A3
With 14 treatment rooms, separate saunas for men and women, a fitness center and full-service hair and nail salon, this spa has all the bases covered. Treatments include the Javanese Lulur, a traditional body cleansing that utilizes turmeric, red rice, fenugreek, jasmine, and ylang ylang.

Mandara Spa Swan and Dolphin
Walt Disney World Dolphin, 1500 Epcot Resorts Boulevard, Lake Buena Vista; tel: 407-934-4772; www.mandaraspa.com; daily 8am–10pm; map p.138 B2
At 12,000sq ft, this retreat inspired by ancient Asian architecture features two interior gardens that make tranquil resting places before and after your treat-

> The Grand Floridian Health Spa has created its own line of grapefruit-flavored skin products.

Above: a tranquil retreat at the Urban spa.

ment. Elemis aromatherapy products are used exclusively.

Ritz-Carlton Spa
Grand Lakes Orlando, 4012 Central Florida Parkway, Orlando; tel: 407-206-2400; www.ritzcarlton.com
The citrus-based treatments at the Ritz sound good enough to eat. Their East Indian Lime Body and Scalp Treatment uses avocado, macadamia, hazelnut oil, wild lime blossom, and other exotic Indian spices to cre-

Left: the perfect antidote to a walk in the parks.

Resembling a late-19th-century country retreat in upstate New York, the spa offers fittingly rustic treatments such as the Maple Sugar Body Polish.

Spa at Rosen Shingle Creek

Shingle Creek Resort, 9939 Universal Boulevard, Orlando; tel: 407-996-9SPA; www.spaat shinglecreek.com; Link: 58; map p.136 B1

Just like its resort, this spa takes its cue from the natural world around it. The Ocoee Body Mask and Calusa Cacoon use the essences of Florida's indigenous plants.

Urban Spa

Eo Inn, 227 North Eola Drive, Orlando; tel: 407-481-8485; www.eoinn.com; daily 9am–6pm; map p.135 C2

This European-style spa comes as a bit of a surprise in Downtown Orlando. It has an extensive list of à la carte services and packages that can be tailored to fill an entire day and include lunch.

ate a balm that is rubbed into your skin to improve circulation.

Shala Salon & Spa at the Peabody Hotel

9801 International Drive, Orlando; tel: 407-248-8009; www.shalasalon.com; Mon–Sat 9am–8pm, Sun 10am–6pm; I-Ride: mainline; map p.136 A1

Shala Salon & Spa; 7226 West Sand Lake Road, Orlando; tel: 407-248-8828; Mon–Sat 9am–8pm, Sun 10am–6pm; Link: 43; map p.136 A2

These two locations of the Shala Salon and Spa offer extensive beauty treatments from haircuts to pedicures aimed at primping executives before conferences. The shorter menu of spa treatments is still enough to help you relax after the meetings, including everything from day packages to facials.

The Spa at Buena Vista Palace

1900 Buena Vista Drive, Lake Buena Vista; tel: 866-397-6516; www.buenavista palace.com; daily 8am–10pm; map p.139 D2

Measuring over 10,000sq ft, this is more than your average resort spa. The menu is equally impressive, with a Pineapple Body Scrub, a full selection of massage techniques, and the unmissable Themed Park Leg Relief Wrap.

Spa at Disney's Saratoga Springs

Saratoga Spring Resort and Spa; tel: 407-827-4455; map p.139 C2

Below: relaxing hard at the Portofino Spa.

Restaurants

Thankfully Orlando's restaurant scene has perked up in recent years, largely due to a crop of hot young chefs who are staking a claim to North America's top tourist market. The bad news – and this pertains mostly to the theme parks, especially Disney – is that food is over-priced and often of poor quality. It's not to say quality can't be had in theme parks. Some places, like Cinderella's Royal Table and the Coral Reef Restaurant, take unique advantage of their park's features to create unforgettable experiences. Here we highlight only the full-service options that are available.

Magic Kingdom

Cinderella's Royal Table
Cinderella's Castle; tel: 407-939-3463; daily B, L, D; $$$; map p.6
Though the food at this restaurant is far below the standard you'd expect at this price, its setting at the heart of Cinderella's Castle cannot be beaten. Children are also given the opportunity to have their picture taken with Cinderella before lunch, and other fairytale princesses pay them a personal visit while they are eating – such a better interaction than most of the meet-and-greet opportunities in the park. In addition to the Fairytale Lunch, there is a Once Upon a Time Breakfast Buffett. The dinner sitting does not include characters. Reservations must be made far in advance.

Tony's Town Square Restaurant
Main Street, U.S.A.; tel: 407-939-

3463; daily L, D; $$; map p.6
With decor inspired by the classic film *Lady and the Tramp*, this restaurant serves up standard Italian fare in a light and airy environment. Be warned of Disney's tomato sauce. This oregano-laden concoction is definitely not to everyone's taste but is served throughout the park, finding its way onto everything from the posh pasta here to kiddie's spaghetti meals in other restaurants.

Epcot

Akershus Royal Banquet Hall
Norway Pavillion; daily B, L, D; $$; map p.10
In addition to its character breakfast featuring Disney princesses in a Norwegian castle setting, this restaurant offers a fine lunch and dinner menu. Guests can choose their main course from a list of Norwegian specialties that include several good fish dishes. Additionally, the smorgasbord of cheeses, pickled fish, and rustic breads is open to all.

Above: Epcot's Italian food is as convincing as its surroundings.

Biergarten Restaurant
Germany Pavilion; daily L, D; $$; map p.10
This buffet-style restaurants set in a dimly lit mock-timber house pays a typically German homage to bratwurst and other stodgy fare. There is, of course, a healthy selection of beers to wash it down with, and the accordion player will catch up with you eventually.

Bistro de Paris
France Pavilion; D daily; $$$; map p.10
The signature restaurant for

Left: the dramatic backdrop in the Coral Reef Restaurant.

and boat ride, its menu includes salads and vegetables grown in The Land greenhouses. The "Full Country Breakfast" stars Mickey, Minnie, and Chip 'n' Dale.

Le Cellier Steakhouse
Canada Pavilion; daily L, D; $$; map p.10

Americans like their steak as much as their northern neighbors, and if you plan on having dinner here you must book in advance even during the slow periods. The wine cellar could make a romantic setting if you are lucky enough to get a table in a quiet corner.

L'Originale Alfredo di Roma Ristorante
Italy Pavilion; daily L, D; $$; map p.10

Colorful, festive offshoot of the famous Roman restaurant. The specialty is fettuccine Alfredo. All pastas are made fresh. Strolling musicians entertain guests.

Nine Dragons Restaurant
China Pavilion; daily L, D; $$; map p.10

Most will be pleased by the cuisine from different Chinese regions, including Mongolia and Szechuan. The menu also features a range of Chinese beers, and the setting is a re-creation of a Chinese palace.

If there is a particular restaurant you'd like to experience at Disney World, book far in advance. There's a reason that Disney takes reservations over a year in advance; during peak season demand easily outweighs supply, and Disney visitors are notorious for their obsessive forward planning. To make a booking, tel: 407-939-3463.

France is poorly appointed, with a dining area that feels not unlike a convention luncheon setting. The lengthy wine list and fine view could help you forget this, but you'd expect more from a Disney restaurant charging this much.

Chefs de France
France Pavilion; daily L, D; $$; map p.10

The more accessible of France's two restaurants, there is nothing pretentious in this restaurant's decor – a faithful re-creation of a typical Parisian café. The cooking may not be up to Michelin-star status, but it is very good, and you get the opportunity to dine under a faux Eiffel Tower.

Coral Reef Restaurant
The Seas with Nemo and Friends; daily L, D; $$$; map p.10

This seafood restaurant is situated alongside the aquarium at The Seas with Nemo and Friends, providing dreamy views into the largest inland saltwater environment ever built, which contains 85 different species of tropical fish. The food is fine dining at Disney's best, and it's hard to beat the setting.

Garden Grill
The Land Pavilion; daily L, D; $$; map p.10

A revolving restaurant overlooking scenic ecosystems

Below: soon to be seen served at the Garden Grill.

Above: just like an old-fashioned drive-in, only in-car activities are much changed.

Restaurant Marrakesh
Morocco Pavilion; daily L, D; $$;
map p.10

After experiencing the fantastic, warren-like architecture of the Morocco pavilion, you can't help but be disappointed by the lack of authenticity once you enter Restaurant Marrakesh. The interior beyond the guest services desk seems bare, and although some of the food excels, most of it is a poor Americanized version of Middle Eastern food. This must be the only Moroccan restaurant in the world without a standard tagine dish. On a more positive note, the live music and belly dancing add a touch of Moroccan flare.

San Angel Inn Restaurante
Mexico Pavillion; daily L, D; $$;
map p.10

Authentic Mexican food served in a very faux environment – under the shadow of a Mayan temple and a smoldering volcano. The dim lighting makes a good option for couples hoping for a bit of romance – an aspect of human experience Disney has yet to turn into a theme park.

Teppanyaki Dining Rooms
Japan Pavilion; L, D daily; $$;
map p.10

Reservations for most meals are necessary to get a seat around one of the five teppanyaki grills. Diners encircle the chef as he creates various stir-fry creations which are shared around the table.

Animal Kingdom

Rainforest Café
Oasis, tel: 939-9100;
www.rainforestcafe.com; daily
L, D; $$; map p.14

This is one of the most highly themed restaurants in Disney, and what an accomplishment. Many will be familiar with this chain and its reliance on animatronic animals and faux decor to re-create a rainforest canopy. Unfortunately, the theme stops at the food. Instead of an iguana burger and plantains, expect typical American food with large portions, and a dessert called the Volcano that is surely a health risk in itself. If you were in any doubt about the chain's true motives, its shop is as large

as the restaurant. Waits of an hour or more are not uncommon without reservations.

Hollywood Studios

50s Prime Time Café
Echo Lake; daily L, D; $; map p.16

This reincarnation of mom's kitchen has a certain fetish appeal. Waiters discipline anyone who does not clean their plate, or is caught with elbows on the table. And at times they behave like mom's children, too, becoming tattle tales and pests just the same. The food is just what you'd expect from mom and includes meatloaf, peas, and indulgent deserts you choose from a retro Viewmaster toy.

Hollywood Brown Derby
Hollywood Boulevard; daily L, D; $$$; map p.16

This re-creation of the legendary Hollywood restaurants features fine food at fine prices. Of course, the only celebrities you are likely to see here are in photographs that adorn the walls.

Mama Melrose's Ristorante Italiano
Streets of America; daily L, D; $$; map p.16

This cozy Italian restaurant serves child-friendly favorites such as pizza and lasagne.

Prices for an average three-course meal with wine:
$ under $20
$$ $20–30
$$$ over $30

Sci-Fi Dine-In Theater
Commissary Lane; daily L, D; $$;
map p.16

This is Hollywood Studio's best dining experience. Every party gets to take a seat in an old Chevy or other vintage car and watch classic sci-fi films on the drive-in screen. The food plays second fiddle to this theme and features burgers, sandwiches, and pasta dishes. Nevertheless, reservations are essential here, even during the slow seasons.

Downtown Disney

Bongos Cuban Café
Westside; daily L, D; $$;
map p.92

The brainchild of pop star Gloria Estefan and her husband Emilio. A giant pineapple sprouting from the roof sets the tone of the place, which throbs with Latin music and brilliant colors. Aficionados of Cuban cuisine may have better luck elsewhere.

Cap'n Jack's Restaurant
Marketplace; daily L, D; $$;
map p.92

This pier-house restaurant features crab, lobster, clams, and oysters, plus plenty of "land lubber" specials. There are some pleasant views of the lake.

Fulton's Crab House
Pleasure Island; daily L, D; $$$;
map p.92

Downtown Disney's lagoon provides berth for this replica of a Mississippi riverboat. Inside is one of Disney's finer fine-dining restaurants. Unsurprisingly, the menu offers a bounty of seafood with a few beef, poultry, and pasta dishes to keep everyone in the party happy. The Alaskan king crab claws are bigger than most men's hands, and there is a decent wine list and a wine selector to help choose the best accompaniment to your meal.

House of Blues
Westside; daily L, D; $$;
map p.92

Founded by actor, comedian, and original Blues Brother Dan Aykroyd and others, and done up like the kind of ramshackle wharfside warehouse you might find in the Mississippi Delta. The food is surprisingly good for a chain operation,

> The lakeside patio at Bongos Cuban Café is a pleasant place to sip a fancy tropical drink.

with spicy southern favorites like fried catfish, seafood gumbo, jambalaya, and bread pudding dribbled with brandy sauce. If you're traveling with kids, consider booking a table for the **Sunday Gospel Brunch**. You'll jump up for Jesus and chow down on all the southern vittles you can eat. It's a soulful way to finish your week at Disney.

Wolfgang Puck
Westside; daily L, D; $$;
map p.92

The cavernous rooms and chatty clientele aren't exactly conducive to an intimate conversation; the atmosphere is all color and energy, with open kitchens, video monitors showing chefs at work, and a bustling wait staff. The menu runs the gamut from sushi and gourmet pizza to lamb chops and seafood, all prepared with the celebrity chef's Californian flair (except perhaps the Wiener schnitzel). The upstairs dining

Below: Bongos Cuban Café gives Downtown Disney a fruity skyline.

About: if visiting from abroad, don't leave Orlando without sampling some Mexican favourites.

room is quite expensive. The downstairs café is cheaper and more casual, and the food is just as tasty.

Planet Hollywood
Westside; tel: 407-939-3463; daily L, D; $$; map p.92

The worldwide restaurant chain launched by Arnold Schwarzenegger, Bruce Willis, Sylvester Stallone, and entrepreneur Robert Earl. Every inch of the dome-shaped dining room is jammed with movie props, memorabilia, and other eye candy. The good news is that the food has improved since the company's brush with bankruptcy in 1999. The bad news? The wait can be terribly long, especially when the theaters let out, so it's sensible to make reservations well in advance.

Portobello Yacht Club
Pleasure Island; daily L, D; $$$; map p.92

First-rate northern Italian cuisine and seafood specialties fill the menu here, while diners cram the floor in a restaurant that could be a fine-dining experience if the spacing wasn't so similar to sitting in a cafeteria.

Rainforest Café
Marketplace; tel: 407-939-3463; daily L, D; $$; map p.92

The smoke you've been seeing billowing in the distance is from a smoldering volcano that sits atop the Rainforest Café, a cavernous restaurant with an extravagant jungle setting. Even with priority seating, you'll have a good long wait. Management hopes you'll spend the time (and at least a few extra dollars) in the adjoining gift shop.

Disney Resort Dining

MAGIC KINGDOM RESORTS

Artist's Point
Wilderness Lodge, 901 Timberline Drive, Lake Buena Vista; daily D; $$$; map p.138 B4

Inspired by America's national-park lodges, this hotel restaurant features salmon, rainbow trout, elk chops, venison, bison, and other hearty dishes associated with the American west. The wine list features labels from the Pacific northwest.

Don't forget to leave a tip when dining out in the United States; servers are paid very little in actual wages, on the assumption that tips will keep them afloat. For large parties and at a few more expensive restaurants, gratuities or a service charge will be added to the bill. If not, leave an additional 15–20 percent tip for good service.

California Grill
Contemporary Resort, 4600 North World Drive; daily D; $$$; map 138 B4

Views of the Magic Kingdom are spectacular from this refined restaurant on the 15th floor of the Contemporary Resort. The menu changes seasonally but usually includes entrées like oak-roasted chicken and pork tenderloin prepared with a light California touch. Don't pass up the appetizers, an eclectic mix of sushi, salads, and pasta. Ask to be seated in time for the fireworks.

Citricos
Grand Floridian Resort and Spa; 4401 Grand Floridian Way, Lake Buena Vista; daily D; $$$; map p.138 A4

Citricos brings a bit of Mediterranean warmth to the Grand Floridian with a selection of food sourced from French, Italian, and Spanish cuisines.

Narcoossee's
Grand Floridian Resort and Spa, 4401 Grand Floridian Way, Lake Buena Vista; daily D; $$$; map p.138 A4

With a sweeping lakeside setting, this is the Grand Floridian's "casual" offering. Its inventive cuisine uses fresh ingredients and lots of seafood. Soft-shell crabs and

Prices for an average three-course meal with wine:
$ under $20
$$ $20–30
$$$ over $30

Prince Edward Island mussels in white wine and garlic are signature dishes.

Victoria and Albert's
Grand Floridian Resort and Spa; 4401 Grand Floridian Way, Lake Buena Vista; daily D; $$$; map p.138 A4
Disney spins a Victorian fantasy at this prix-fixe restaurant. The seven-course meal is served by a white-gloved butler and maid (Albert and Victoria) in a romantic, domed dining room. The menu features some of the finest Continental cuisine in town. Very expensive but, fans say, worth the money.

EPCOT RESORTS
ESPN Sports Club
Disney's BoardWalk; daily L, D; $$$; map p.138 B2
Jocks will love this theme restaurant crammed with all things sporty, including more than 70 television screens; there's even one in the restroom, lest you miss a minute of the big game. Bring a big appetite. Entrées, including hamburgers, hot dogs, sirloin, and grilled chicken, are oversized. Desserts are big and yummy.

Flying Fish Café
Disney's BoardWalk; daily L, D; $$$; map p.138 B2
One of Disney's best restaurants, in a whimsical setting with a busy stage kitchen. It serves potato-wrapped yellowtail snapper and other creative dishes. There's chocolate lava cake for dessert.

Il Mulino New York Trattoria
Swan Hotel, 1200 Epcot Resorts Boulevard; daily D; $$$; map p.138 B2
Is this the classiest restaurant at Disney World? The illuminated wine bar is tops for sure, and it has a good selection of fine wines. Food features recipes based on classic Italian bistro recipes. The seafood dishes stand out the most.

Kimono's
Swan Hotel, 1200 Epcot Resorts Boulevard; daily D; $$$; map p.138 B2
As much a retreat as a restaurant, the sushi chefs here are not shy and are happy to prepare their beautiful creations in front of your eyes. For those who prefer their fish cooked, there are hot dishes and tempura available as well. The class doesn't last all night – karaoke begins in the evening.

Todd English's bluezoo
Dolphin Hotel, 1200 Epcot Resorts Boulevard; daily D; $$$; map p.138 B2
Presentation is king at this fine-dining restaurant, from the sleek backlit bar and minimalist design to the simply decorous plates of seafood with a wedge of lemon. There is a kids' menu here, but do yourself a favor and leave the little ones behind so you can enjoy this very grown-up restaurant.

ANIMAL KINGDOM RESORTS
Jiko – The Cooking Place
Animal Kingdom Lodge, 2901 Osceola Parkway, Lake Buena Vista; daily D; $$$; map p.138 A1
An African sunset sets the color scheme for this romantic restaurant, but the cuisine takes its tone more from Europe and India than the African savannah.

Celebration and Kissimmee

Azteca's Restaurant
809 North Main Street, Kissimmee; tel: 407-933-8155; www.aztecasmexrestaurant.com; Mon–Thur 11am–9.30pm, Fri and Sat 11am–10.30pm, Sun 11am–8pm; $$; Link: 4; map p.18
There's nothing pretentious about this local favorite. The walls are decorated with eclectic hangings, and the menu includes Mexican standards such as burritos, enchiladas, and nachos for starters. All Mexican beers are available.

Café D'Antonio Ristorante Celebration
691 Front Street, Celebration; tel: 407-566-2233; www.antoniosonline.com; daily L, D; $$$; map p.18
This upscale Italian restaurant serves an extensive

Below: a Spanish paella from Columbia Restaurant, *see p.104.*

Above: the classy interior of Celebration's Columbia Restaurant.

This little bit of England has nestled quietly into Disney's hometown. A combination teahouse, deli, and restaurant, it is open all day for quick cups of Earl Grey to Champagne Tea. Live music plays most weekend evenings.

Universal Studios

Finnegan's Bar and Grill
New York; tel: 407-224-3613; daily L, D; $$; map p.20

Meant to be a hometown Irish bar in New York City, Finnegan's has very friendly wait staff and serves fish and chips, corned beef, and, of course, Irish stew. Guinness is on tap.

Lombard's Seafood Grille
San Francisco/Amity; tel: 407-224-3613; daily L, D; $$; map p.20

Lombard's serves the best food at Universal Studios. The clam chowder pays homage to the east coast, while the fresh seafood and tasty pastas have a more Californian feel. Either way, you're likely to leave happy.

Islands of Adventure

Confisco Grille
Port of Entry; tel: 407-224-4012; daily B, L, D; $$; map p.22

Decorated as an exotic wharfside tavern, Confisco Grille offers ethnic dishes ranging from fajitas and pad

selection of pastas but an even wider selection of meat and chicken dishes, with several veal selections. Its wine list includes fine Italian wines and a healthy selection from California. There is also a location in Maitland that includes a deli and café *(see p.69).*

Columbia Restaurant
649 Front Street, Celebration; tel: 407-566-1505; www.columbiarestaurant.com; daily L, D; $$$; map p.18

The Columbia restaurant chain dates back to 1905 when its original outlet opened in Tampa's Ybor City. This classy restaurant serves Spanish cuisine that has amalgamated Cuban and Mexican influences while in Florida. The result for anyone who likes a bit of spice is a winner. There is flamenco dancing in the evening.

Market Street Café
701 Front Street, Celebration; tel: 407-566-1144; daily B, L, D; $$; map p.18

This classic American diner serves breakfast all day, which includes everything from a posh crab omelette to

buttermilk pancakes. Dinner selections are varied and include burgers, meatloaf, and stir-fry. There is also an old-fashioned soda fountain serving ice cream treats.

Plantation Room
Celebration Hotel, 700 Bloom Street, Celebration; tel: 407-566 6002; www.celebration hotel.com; daily B, L, D; $$$; map p.18

Affordable, gourmet, nouvelle Florida cuisine, including master dinners featuring everything from 'gator to kangaroo. Breakfast is lovely and excellent value.

Sherlocks
715 Bloom Street, Suite 130, Celebration; tel: 407-566-1866; www.sherlocksgroup.com; Mon–Thur 8.30am–9pm, Fri 8.30am–10pm, Sat 10am–10pm and Sun 10am–9pm; $$; map p.18

Below: a deliciously citrus concoction.

Prices for an average three-course meal with wine:
$ under $20
$$ $20–30
$$$ over $30

Another thing you'll find at Universal Studios that Disney would never consider is a happy hour at Finnegan's Bar and Grill.

Above: the feel of down-home luxury at the Plantation Room.

thai to barbecued ribs. Drinks are available at the Backwater Bar, which has a small patio perfect for people-watching. The restaurant also hosts the daily character breakfast.

Mythos

Lost Continent; tel: 407-224-4012; daily L, D; $$$; map p.22
The park's best restaurant is ensconced in a regally appointed cavern with sculpted walls, purple uphol-stery, and lagoon views. Entrées include wood-roasted lobster with wild mushroom risotto, cedar-planked salmon with orange horseradish mashed potatoes, and wood-fired pizza, plus other child-friendly dishes.

CityWalk

Bob Marley A Tribute to Freedom

Tel: 407-224-3663; daily L, D; $$; map p.50
You can chow down on yucca chips, jerk chicken, and plenty of Red Stripe beer while jammin' to reggae. The exterior is modeled after Marley's home in Kingston, Jamaica. Inside, photos and other artifacts chronicle his life and career. Live bands perform nightly on the court-yard stage.

Bubba Gump Shrimp Company

Tel: 407-224-3663; daily L, D; $$; map p.50
For many, Bubba Gump is the last character they'd like to have dinner with, having spent more than enough time with this annoying "life is a box of chocolates" character in the overlong film. But where there's a celluloid suc-

cess in the US, a themed restaurant is not far behind. The food here is mostly shrimp-based and of the quality you'd expect from a roadside café in Mobile for at least half the price.

Emeril's Restaurant Orlando

Tel: 407-224-3663; daily L, D; $$$; map p.50
Featuring the creations of television chef Emeril Lagasse. Assertive Creole flavors bubble up through artfully prepared specialties like grilled pork chop with caramelized sweet potatoes. Wine connoisseurs can choose from more than 10,000 bottles. The desserts are equally glorious; homey favorites like root beer floats and banana cream pie become decadent master-pieces.

Hard Rock Café Orlando

Tel: 407-224-3663; daily L, D; $$; map p.50
When it comes to theme restaurants, the big daddy of 'em all is the Hard Rock Café. With seating for 600 in the restaurant and 3,000 in the concert hall, this is the largest Hard Rock in the world, and, like its humbler brethren, its walls are plas-tered with gold records, album covers, flashy cos-tumes, and instruments that have been strummed and drummed by some of the rock world's biggest names. A pink Cadillac revolves over the bar; a Sistine Chapel-like mural featuring a heavenly host of dead rock stars adorns the ceiling; and stained-glass panels pay trib-ute to a trinity of rock le-gends – Elvis Presley, Chuck

Below: CityWalk's most exclusive restaurant.

Above: sushi is popular in trendy restaurants.

Berry, and Jerry Lee Lewis. It's a bit much to take in over a meal, which is why the Hard Rock offers free tours in the afternoon.

Jimmy Buffet's Margaritaville
Tel: 407-224-3663; daily L, D; $$; map p.50

For a laid-back beach bum, Jimmy Buffet is quite the entrepreneur. Decked out in beachy, tropical style, this restaurant leans toward Caribbean flavors – conch fritters, seafood chowder, grilled fish – with a sprinkling of American standards, including the inevitable "cheeseburger in paradise."

Latin Quarter
Tel: 407-224-3663; daily L, D; $$; map p.50

Both the food and the music are spicy at the Latin Quarter, dedicated to the culture and cuisine of 21 Latin American nations. After dinner, an orchestra and dance troupe take the stage. Dance instructors initiate neophytes into the wonders of merengue, salsa, and the mambo.

NASCAR Sports Grille
Tel: 407-224-3663; daily L, D; $$; map p.50

Anchoring the far end of the Plaza, near the bridge to Universal Studios, is NASCAR, a testament to the popularity of stock-car racing. Fans munch on chicken wings, chili, and burgers in a boisterous room with video games and live acts, where every square inch is plastered with racing paraphernalia. There are even a couple of racing cars suspended from the ceiling.

NBA City
Tel: 407-224-3663; daily L, D; $$; map p.50

NBA City, if you hadn't guessed, is the restaurant with the statue of a basketball player towering over the entrance. Inside is hoopster heaven, with skill games, shrines to b-ball stars, and a battery of video monitors replaying the game's greatest moments. There are tasty grilled salmon, roasted chicken, and strip steak, as well as kid-friendly choices like burgers, pizza, and sandwiches. The milkshakes are a slam dunk; for nearly a tenner, they ought to be.

Pastamoré
Tel: 407-224-3663; daily L, D; $$; map p.50

Pastamoré serves up abundant portions of eggplant parmigiana, veal Marsala, and a dozen varieties of pizza and pasta. An option to dine family-style lets you taste a little bit of everything, including the *dolci assortiti*, a selection of yummy desserts.

Pat O'Brien's Orlando
Tel: 407-224-3663; daily L, D; $$; map p.50

An older crowd inhabits Pat O'Brien's, a replica of a landmark New Orleans watering hole. The singalong crowd loves the dueling pianos, and foodies enjoy jambalaya, muffeletta, and other Big Easy specialties. Wash it down with a Hurricane, O'Brien's signature rum drink.

Universal Studios Resorts

Bice Ristorante
Portofino Bay Hotel; 5601 Universal Boulevard, Orlando; tel: 407-503-1415; daily D; $$$; map p.136 A3

The clean, simple lines of this upscale trattoria make way for a fine Italian dining experience. The Bice chain began in Milan and is famed as much for its hospitality as its food.

Emeril's Tchoup Chop
Royal Pacific Resort, 6300 Hollywood Way, Orlando; tel: 407-503-3000; daily L, D; $$$; map p.136 A3

Emeril's second restaurant on Universal Orlando's property is dedicated to the delicate flavours of Asian and Polynesian cuisine. The restaurant's seductive decor is created using palm trees, bamboo, and waterfalls.

Prices for an average three-course meal with wine:
$ under $20
$$ $20–30
$$$ over $30

With three bars and one margarita-spewing volcano, Jimmy Buffett's Margaritaville keeps customers well oiled whether they're there to eat or not.

Mama Della's Ristorante
Portofino Bay Hotel; 5601 Universal Boulevard, Orlando; tel: 407-503-3463; daily D; $$$; map p.136 A3

As heavy on themes as on the stomach. The hearty Italian fare is accompanied by fine wines and strolling entertainment, including singers and guitarists. Mama herself makes an appearance, too, insisting that everyone eats up.

Palm Restaurant
Hard Rock Hotel, 5800 Universal Boulevard, tel: 407-503-7256; daily D; $$$; map p.136 A3

Carnivores can slice into slabs of beef at this knock-off of the famous New York steakhouse – a favorite with the meat and martini crowd. Like the original, there are celebrity caricatures on the wall and a whiff of testosterone in the air.

International Drive and Lake Buena Vista

Bergamo's Italian Restaurant
Festival Bay Mall, 5250 International Drive, Orlando; tel: 407-352-3805; daily 5–10pm; $$$; I-Ride: mainline; map p.136 B3

Bergamo's has earned kudos for an attractive ambience and beautifully-prepared pasta, steak, and seafood (thankfully not overcooked, as is so often the case in Orlando). It also has the largest list of Italian wines in the city, and the wait staff, all talented vocalists, sing everything from operatic arias to Neopolitan folk songs every evening.

B-Line Diner
Peabody Hotel, 9801 International Drive, Orlando; tel: 407-345-4460; 24hrs; $$; I-Ride: mainline; map p.136 B1

A cozy, 1950s-style diner that's open 24 hours a day, it features thick sandwiches, griddle cakes, and a jukebox with vintage tunes. The corned-beef hash and eggs for breakfast is about as good as slop can get.

Bola Ristorante
8148 International Drive, Orlando; tel: 407-345-8884; www.bolaristorante.com; daily 11.30am–2pm, 4–11pm; $$$; I-Ride: mainline; map p.136 A2

This Italian restaurant has the classiest interior on I-Drive, and would not look out of place on South Beach. The cuisine is classic Italian fare, with a lighter touch. They take pride in creating simple dishes using the finest ingredients. Their bar has a happy hour between four and seven, with a half-priced drinks and appetizers.

Cala Bella
Rosen Shingle Creek, 9939 Universal Boulevard, Orlando; tel: 407-996-3663; www.calabella restaurant.com; $$; Link: 58; map p.136 B1

Located at the out-of-the-way Rosen Shingle Creek Resort, this Italian restaurant has a reputation for well-presented basic Italian dishes like risottos, fresh pastas, clams, steaks, seafood, and Tuscan bean soup.

The Capital Grille
Pointe Orlando, 9101 International Drive, Orlando; tel: 407-370-4392; www.capital grille.com; Mon–Fri 11.30am–3pm, Sun–Thur 5–10pm, Fri and Sat 5–11pm; $$$; I-Ride: mainline; map p.136 A1

Dry-aged steak is the centerpiece of the Capital Grille's menu, one that is not kind to vegetarians, but does offer a few seafood options. The wine cellar has over 5,000 bottles from around the world.

Capriccio Grill Italian Steakhouse
Peabody Orlando, 9801 International Drive, Orlando; tel: 407-345-4450; www.peabody orlando.com; $$$; I-Ride: mainline; map p.136 A1

A show kitchen is the center of attention at this upscale, marble-clad restaurant specializing in gourmet pizza, grilled meats and seafood, heaping bowls of pasta, and other Italian dishes.

Ciao Italia Ristorante Italiano
6149 Westwood Boulevard, Orlando; tel: 407-354-0770; www.ciaoitaliaonline.com; $$$; I-Ride: mainline; map p.139 E4

Below: one of many good restaurants at Pointe Orlando.

Above: the Peabody's famous mascots.

This family-run restaurant has a warm, welcoming setting combined with fine food. The standard menu is basic, but evening specials offer more adventurous entrées, and the wine list has a fine selection of Italian wines.

Dux

Peabody Hotel, 9801 International Drive, Orlando; tel: 407-345-4550; Tue–Sat D only; $$$; I-Ride: mainline; map p.136 A1

Elegant restaurant with innovative American cuisine. Starters include Osetra caviar and lobster and potato salad. Entrées focus on fish, but there are steaks and lamb for those craving meat. One of Orlando's finest dining experiences.

Hanamizuki Japanese Restaurant

8255 International Drive, Suite 136, Orlando; tel: 407-363-7200; www.hanamizuki.uk; $$; I-Ride: mainline; map p.136 A2

Tucked away in the Goodings Plaza is this wonderful Japanese restaurant. The head chef's skills are so advanced he has even been given the honor of serving the Emperor of Japan at his summer retreat. The food and drink, from sushi to sake, is as authentic as you'll find in central Florida, and the relaxing minimalistic decor is a welcome retreat from chaotic I-Drive.

A Land Remembered

Rosen Shingle Creek, 9939 Universal Boulevard, Orlando; tel: 866-996-9939; www.land rememberedrestaurant.com; $$$; Link: 58; map p.136 B1

This steakhouse is named after a novel written by Patrick Smith, which focused on Florida's history and landscapes. So it should be no surprise that alligator appears on the menu. Otherwise, the fine-dining menu is varied, with several seafood options available for those not wanting steak. The wine list will leave no one disappointed.

Ming Court

9188 International Drive, Orlando; tel: 407-351-9988; www.ming-court.com; daily 11am–2.30pm, 4.30–11.30pm; $$; I-Ride: mainline; map p.136 A1

Interior koi ponds and gardens set the stage at this fine Chinese restaurant. The chefs cook up specialties of several provinces and even produce fine sushi, as well as a delectable dim sum menu. Ask for a table near the open kitchen.

Prices for an average three-course meal with wine:
$ under $20
$$ $20–30
$$$ over $30

Norman's

The Ritz-Carlton Grande Lakes, 4012 Central Florida Parkway, Orlando; tel: 407-393-4333; www.normans.com; Sun–Thur 6pm–10pm, Fri and Sat 6pm–10.30; $$$

Norman Van Aken's New World Cuisine is defined by dishes created when European tradition encounters the native cultures of the Caribbean, Central America, and Florida. Sommeliers offer advice on which vintages best accompany these dishes, and the setting is elegance all the way.

The Oceanaire Seafood Room

Pointe Orlando, 9101 International Drive, Suite 1002, Orlando; tel: 407-363-4801; www.theoceanaire.com; Sun–Thur 5–10 pm, Fri–Sat 5–11pm; $$$; I-Ride: mainline; map p.136 A1

Decorated like a 1930s ocean liner, this sleek diner serves "ultra-fish" seafood, which means that it has arrived that day and was probably in the sea the day before. Such ideals deserve celebration, especially in a city where such sourcing of ingredients often plays second fiddle to grand themes. Hence the menu changes daily, but often includes oysters, simple and tasty fish entrées, and a fine wine

No duck is served at any of the Peabody's restaurants, in honour of the hotel's famous mascots.

list with stewards to guide your selection. Still, it's a pity that in the heart of Florida so much is flown in from New England and Alaska instead of making the best of the bounty of two nearby coasts.

Primo
The Ritz-Carlton Grande Lakes, 4012 Central Florida Parkway, Orlando; tel: 407-393-4444; www.primorestaurant.com; Mon–Sun 6–10pm; $$$
Chef Melissa Kelly creates this "sensible" Italian menu based upon locally sourced ingredients, making the most of the varied citrus fruits and seafood available in Florida.

Venetian Room
Caribe Royale, 8101 World Center Drive, Orlando; tel: 407-238-8060; Tue–Sat 6pm–10pm; jackets suggested; www.the venetianroom.com; $$$; Link: 304; map p.139 D2
The Caribe Royale's flagship restaurant adds a touch of class to this corporate hotel. The fine-dining menu here features European favourites such as foie gras and cheese platters, with an extensive

wine list containing some of California's most renowned winemakers.

SeaWorld

Seafire Inn Restaurant
daily L, D; $$; map p.26
This sprawling restaurant serves Caribbean-style food during the daily Music Maestro lunch show. Reservations are required for the Makahiki Luau, a Polynesian-themed dinner theater.

Sharks Underwater Grill
Near Sharks Encounter; daily L, D; $$$; map p.26
Set beside the enormous Sharks Encounter aquarium: one entire wall of the Underwater Grill's dining room is exposed to the tank, letting you sit in awe of the magnificent creatures swimming past. The food here, mostly seafood, is exquisite; the restaurant can easily produce one of the of the best meals you'll have at a theme park.

Downtown and Loch Haven Park

The Beacon
The Sanctuary, 100 South Eola; tel: 407-841-5444; www.beacon orlando.com; Sun–Mon 4–10pm, Tue–Wed 4–11pm, Thur–Sat 4pm–1am, bar open daily until 2am, brunch Sat & Sun 11am–4pm; $$$; map p.28

This trendy tapas bar has breathed new life into the nightlife scene of Thornton Park, though you have to have a thick wallet to enjoy its extensive wine list, chic interior, and gourmet tapas. The place to see Orlando's upper crust.

The Boheme
Grand Bohemian Hotel, 325 South Orange Avenue, Orlando; tel: 407-313-9000; www.the bohme.com; daily 6am–2.30pm, Sun 6am–10.30am, Sun–Thur 5–10.30pm, Fri–Sat 5–11.30pm; $$$; Link: 3, 6, 7, 11, 13, 18, 51; map p.135 C2
This is one of Orlando's best restaurants, and as each year passes another award is received. A recent addition, the Bohemian Wine Room, allows parties of up to 14 guests to enjoy a private dining room and exclusive service for the evening.

Gargi's Lakeside Italian Ristorante
1414 North Orange Avenue, Orlando; tel: 407-894-7907; www.gargislakeside.com; Mon–Fri 11.30am–3.30pm, Mon–Thur 5–10pm, Fri–Sat 5–11pm, Sun 11.30–9pm; $$; Link: 1, 2, 9; map p.135 C3
Located on Lake Ivanhoe in the heart of Downtown Orlando, this family-run restaurant has grown over the years from a tiny bistro.

Below: the Sharks Underwater Grill's infamous voyeurs.

The menu features veal, steaks, and seafood, all served with fresh pasta. In addition to a sturdy wine list, there is a wide selection of martinis to choose from.

The Globe
27 Wall Street Plaza, Orlando; tel: 407-849-9904; café 11am–11pm, bar until 2am; $$; Link: 3, 6, 7, 11, 13, 18, 51; map p.135 C2

As it's located in Downtown's

Left: the Beacon, a trendy outpost in Thornton Park.

Wall Street Plaza nightlife area, The Globe serves two purposes: a quick bite for office workers and a quick lining of pizza, sandwiches, or salads before heading on for more serious drinking elsewhere. There are sushi and cocktail specials Mon–Fri for happy hour, when live music is played on the patio.

The Harp Restaurant
25 South Magnolia Avenue, Orlando; tel: 407-481-2927; www.harpandcelt.com; Mon–Fri L, Wed–Sat D; $$$; map p.135 C2

Could this be Orlando's first gastropub? The attached **Celt Irish Pub** has a lively atmosphere, while The Harp serves meaty entrées from a limited menu in sedate surrounds. The prices are far too high for pub grub, but neither the atmosphere nor the food exceed those standards.
SEE ALSO BARS AND CAFÉS, P.52

Harvey's Bistro
390 North Orange Avenue, Orlando; tel: 407-246-6560; www.harveysbistro.com; Mon–Thur 11.30am–10pm, Fri 11.30am–11pm, Sat 6–11pm; $$$; Link: 3, 6, 7, 11, 13, 18, 51; map p.135 C2

A little European style goes a

long way at this welcoming bistro, popular with business lunchers and nighttime revelers. Even pot roast and meatloaf are something special, not to mention more ambitious choices such as seared calf liver, crab cakes, roasted duck, and a variety of nicely done pasta dishes.

HUE Restaurant
629 East Central Boulevard, Orlando; tel: 407-849-1800; www.huerestaurant.com; Sun–Wed 3–11, Thur–Sat 3pm–12am; $$$; Link: 5; map p.135 C2

HUE makes the most of local produce in creating familiarly American fare such as wood-grilled filet mignon. The designer interior has a cozy, Scandinavian vibe, with crisp lines accented by warm lighting and candles. The happy hour is very popular.

Little Saigon
1106 East Colonial Drive, Orlando; tel: 407-423-8539; www.littlesaigonrestaurant.com; daily 10am–9pm; $; Link: 28, 29; map p.135 C2

This no-nonsense family-run restaurant is a welcome addition to a town that celebrates simulation over authenticity. Traditional Vietnamese dishes range from delicate spring rolls and rice noodles to big bowls of soup and fiery stir-fries.

White Wolf Café
1829 North Orange Avenue, tel: 407-895-5590; www.whitewolf cafe.com; Mon 11am–9pm, Tue–Thur 11am–10pm, Fri–Sat 11am–11pm; $; Link: 1, 2, 9; map p.135 C3

This tiny slice of Bohemia is a breath of fresh air in theme-

Below: several Vietnamese restaurants operate along East Colonial Drive.

Prices for an average three-course meal with wine:
$ under $20
$$ $20–30
$$$ over $30

We've selected some of Winter Park's best restaurants for our listings, but if you take the time to stroll Park Avenue you may discover a favorite of your own – the choice, especially for Orlando, is astounding.

crazed Orlando. The service isn't exactly snappy, but the atmosphere is friendly, and the menu – ranging from egg salad sandwiches to wild mushroom lasagne – has enough creative quirks to sustain your interest.

Winter Park and Maitland

Antonio's la Fiamma
611 South Orlando Avenue, 2nd floor, Maitland; tel: 407-645-5523; www.antoniosonline.com; Mon–Fri 11.30–2.30, Mon–Sat 5–10pm; $$$; Link: 1, 2, 9; map p.135 C4

Another branch of the fine Antonio's restaurant chain serving pastas, risottos, and authentic Italian meat and fish entrées.

Brio Tuscan Grille
480 North Orlando Avenue, Suite 108, Winter Park; tel: 407-622-5611; www.brioitalian.com; Sun–Thur 11am–10pm, Fri–Sat 11am–11pm; $$; Link: 39; map p.135 D4

This dark-wood-lined Italian chain restaurant could make a good setting for a romantic evening, but one suspects business lunches are more common in this branch, part of the Winter Park Village shopping complex. The menu emphasis is on pork and steaks, but there are hand-tossed pizzas and other lighter touches available for vegetarians or children.

Café de France
526 Park Avenue, South Winter Park; tel: 407-647-1869; www.lecafedefrance.com; Tue–Sat 11.30am–2.30pm, 6–10pm; $$$; map p.135 D4

Start your meal with foie gras, escargot or the daily selection of pâté before enjoying a fine selection of soups and salads and entrées that include lamb, pork, and a fish of the day. A fine wine list is available to accompany your meal.

Houston's
215 South Orlando Avenue, Winter Park; tel: 407-740-4005; www.hillstone.com; $$$; Sun–Thur 11am–10pm, Fri–Sat 11am–11pm; Link: 39; map p.135 D4

You are not likely to stumble across this restaurant, as it is tucked away from Orlando Avenue with not much else around it to draw visitors. This makes its setting on the edge of one of Winter Park's numerous lakes feel even more secluded. The menu varies from five-star burgers costing an arm to gourmet steaks and seafood.

Luma on Park
290 South Park Avenue, Winter Park; tel: 407-599-4111; www.lumaonpark.com; Mon–Thur 5.30–10pm, Fri and Sat 5.30–11pm, Sun 5.30–9pm, lounge opens from 4pm daily; $$$; map p.135 D4

This is perhaps the finest din-ing experience in the buzzing Park Avenue restaurant scene. The menu features a lot of seafood, from scallops to barramundi, and there are steaks and chops, too. The wine list consists of boutique winemakers, mostly from California, and there is a "flight" available that provides samples of their bottles. Uniquely, half-glasses are available for those who would like to change wines for each course yet remain upright.

Space Coast

Cocoa Beach Pier, 401 Meade Avenue, Cocoa Beach, ½ mile north of SR 520, off A1A; tel: 321-783-7549; daily L, D; $–$$$

You could do a lot worse than ending your trip to the Space Coast on the pier at Cocoa Beach. Walk to the end of the pier and you can see the launch pads with your naked eye. It's no secret that this is prime launch-viewing real estate. On the pier itself are three places to eat: the Atlantic Grille is the fanciest option, but any of the choices affords a great view of the Atlantic and the surfers trying to tame it.

Below: rough and ready restaurant with a view that can't be beat from Cocoa Beach Pier.

Shopping

In Orlando, shopping isn't merely about buying stuff, it's just as much about "retail entertainment." Extravagant malls anchor either end of International Drive, and become destinations in themselves in other areas of the city. Specialty shops abound here, especially along the cozy main street of Winter Park, but you'll also find factory outlets which offer enormous savings on everything from sporting goods to designer clothing. Of course, there is no shortage of shops selling themed memorabilia, but there are even a few places where you can get Disney souvenirs at a discount.

What to Buy

If you are into kitsch – plastic flamingo ashtrays, canned sunshine, orange perfume, and the like – you will find Orlando's myriad gift shops a veritable treasure house, and you won't need our help in finding one as they are on nearly every corner.

There are also homegrown souvenirs like oranges, tangerines, limes, kumquats, and grapefruits, which can be shipped home for a small fee. But if you look a little harder, Florida also has an array of quality goods to take home from a trip. There are shops worth seeking out that sell designer clothing at factory prices, fascinating examples of Art Deco and old Floridian antiques, and Native American crafts.

Theme Parks

MAGIC KINGDOM
Main Street Watchmaker
Main Street, U.S.A.
Located on the right side of Main Street, U.S.A. as you enter the park, this classy shop sells designer watches and clocks that are filled with Disney characters. One of the only places in "the Kingdom" to get a posh souvenir.

EPCOT
Mitsukoshi Department Store
Japan
You could easily forget about the rest of Epcot once you enter this shop. At least that's the case for anyone with a liking for finely finished, delicate sushi-serving sets, samurai swords, or paper lanterns.
Yong Feng Shangdian Department Store
China
This fantastic emporium of all things Chinese is the best shopping spot in Epcot. Fine jade figurines and silk robes are just some of the goods on offer.

HOLLYWOOD STUDIOS
Sid Cahuenga's One of a Kind
Hollywood Boulevard
One of the few retail spaces in any of the theme parks that sells something truly unique. Sid's crowded collection of motion-picture mem-

Above: Cocoa Beach's most famous store.

orabilia includes everything from autographed photographs and vintage movie posters to animation stills from classic Disney pictures. A great place to browse, even if the prices are a bit steep for most wallets.

DOWNTOWN DISNEY
Art of Disney
Marketplace
This is your chance to purchase genuine original cells of Disney's animated films. The price isn't cheap, but it is artwork well worth investing in.

Left: Mainstreet, U.S.A. is lined with stores selling everything from standard souvenirs to classic timepieces.

better plan would be to ignore the park's shops and come here, once.

ISLANDS OF ADVENTURE
All the Books You Can Read
Seuss Landing

Finding every Seuss book in print, in more than one language, is a challenge, and this shop really is a one-of-a-kind for parents or collectors wanting to find the more unique Seuss creations for their child.

Comic Book Shop
Marvel Super Hero Island

For those who grew up reading about the adventures of Marvel's super heroes, this store will make a sweet walk down memory lane with action figures, vintage editions, and recent creations all on sale.

KENNEDY SPACE CENTER
Space Shop

Most parks' big shops offer items you can find in any decent shopping mall, but the KSC shop is the largest store in the world devoted to NASA memorabilia. From space ice cream

---

Most Floridians do their shopping in malls, which contain the usual mix of department stores, boutiques, chain stores, and one-of-a-kind shops. Hours vary, but most shopping centers are open seven days a week.

Disney's Days of Christmas
Marketplace

This shop sells everything Christmas all year round. Few can pass up the opportunity to get a unique tree decoration to commemorate their time in Disney World.

Lego Imagination Center
Marketplace

More creative children will welcome this opportunity to build and destroy instead of purchase and unwrap. In addition to selling every conceivable Lego set, this store doubles as an enormous Lego play area, with children free to make anything they choose out of the buckets of bricks left at their disposal.

Once Upon A Toy
Marketplace

This store is devoted solely to toys, both vintage and modern. Interactive exhibits let you get more involved in making your purchase, and there are classic board games for sale here that have been given a unique Disney-fication.

World of Disney
Marketplace

If you've been spending your vacation exploring Disney World, by the time you get here you will think you've seen all there is to see in terms of memorabilia. But there may be something that still surprises you in this, the largest of all Disney shops. A

Below: gift shops, many of them of dubious quality, are ubiquitous in Orlando's main tourist areas.

Above: sunwear is available everywhere.

to souvenir shirts and space suits for children, this really is a unique place to buy great space gear.

Shopping Malls

Festival Bay
5250 International Drive, Orlando; tel: 800-481-1944 or 407-351-7718; www.shop festivalbaymall.com; Mon–Sat 10am–9pm, Sun 11am–7pm; I-Ride: mainline; map p.136 B3
Festival Bay is more than an outlet mall. It contains some of the heaviest-themed stores in the area, including **Vans Skatepark** (tel: 407-351-3881 for bookings), with a 25,000sq-ft street course, a **Ron Jon Surf Shop** (tel: 407-481-255), and accompanying Surf Park to open soon. There is also the enormous **Bass Pro Shop** (tel: 407-563-5200) for your fishing gear and a **Sheplers** (tel: 407-563-1063) outlet for your western wear.

Florida Mall
8001 South Orange Blossom Trail, Orlando; tel: 407-851-6255; Mon–Sat 10am–9pm, Sun noon–6pm, some restaurants and department stores stay open later; Link: 4, 7, 37 42, 43, 52; map p.137 D2

A destination in itself, the Florida Mall is too big to be explored in one day. For those who feel that is a challenge, be prepared to encounter, for a few minutes each, six department stores, 18 jewelry stores, 22 shore stores, over 53 clothing stores, and one hotel. Enjoy the smell of your burning plastic.

Lake Buena Vista Factory Stores
15657 State Road 535, Orlando; tel: 407-238-9301; www.lbvfs.com; Mon–Sat 10am–9pm, Sun 10am–6pm; Link: 300; map p.139 D1
When faced with so many supermalls in Orlando, it's easy to overlook this smallish strip mall located east of I-4, but its bargains would stand out anywhere else. The Gap and Reebok outlets provide some of the best discounts in Orlando, while the S&K Men's Store has unbelievable bargains for tailor-made men's suits, shirts, and pants.

Mall at Millenia
4200 Conroy Road, Orlando; tel: 407-363-3555; www.mallat millenia.com; Mon–Sat 10am–9pm, Sun noon–7pm; Link: 24, 40, 305; map p.136 B3
Anchored by Neiman Marcus, Bloomingdale's, and Macy's department stores, this mall has over 100 other stores. There are plenty of familiar names such as Gap and Burberry to choose from, and a few unique stores to make things more interesting. In addition to the standard food court fare, there are a few more upscale chains if you'd like to have a bit of luxury with your post-shopping refreshments.

Old Town
5770 West Irlo Bronson Memorial Highway (US 192), Kissimmee; tel: 407-396-48888 or 800-843-4202; www.old-town.com; daily 10am–11pm, rides and pubs stay open later; Link: 55; map p.139 C1
Old Town has little in the way of shops that would pull in the customers. Most are attracted by the rides, which look better when you're driving by at 40mph than when you are standing next to them. The area is also popular at night, when its pubs attract a large British expat crowd.

Pointe Orlando
9101 International Drive, Orlando; tel: 407-248-2838; www.pointeorlando.com; Mon–Sat 10am–10pm, Sun 11am–9pm, some restaurants open later; I-Ride: mainline; map p.136 A1
This is the central shopping and dining venue along International Drive. Shops range from Chico's (tel: 407-352-4780) stylish, middle-of-the

Recently developed central Florida may not seem the best place to hunt for antiques, but a surprising number of shops operate on Antique Road, otherwise known as Orange Avenue in Downtown Orlando.

road womenswear and Gray Fifth Avenue's (tel: 800-549-4497) fine male fashion, to an Armani Exchange (tel: 407-352-3311) offering cut-rate deals on designer goods, and the unique Bimini Shoes (tel: 407-354-9898) with "fashion for your feet."

Premium Outlets

8200 Vineland Avenue, Orlando; tel: 407-238-7787; www.premiumoutlets.com/orlando; Mon–Sat 10am–11pm, Sun 10am–9pm; Link: 303; I-Ride: main and greenlines; map p.139 D3

With 110 discount stores, Premium Outlets is one of the largest malls in Florida. Designer names include Polo Ralph Lauren (tel: 407-239-7656), Hugo Boss (tel: 407-465-0660), Dior (tel: 407-239-0090), Burberry (tel: 407-238-7777), Armani (tel: 407-550-4490), Diesel (tel: 407-239-6267), Calvin Klein (tel: 407-465-0030), and Gap (tel: 407-238-1514). Sportswear can be found at Nike (tel: 407-239-2662), Adidas (tel: 407-239-2836), Reebok (tel: 407-239-8901), and Puma (tel: 407-239-6211). Little Me (tel: 407-239-9991) and OshKosh B'Gosh (tel: 407-239-4666) cater to children. The Samsonite store (tel: 407-465-1443) offers some savings on exclusive luggage. There is a simple food court if you need refreshment.

Prime Outlets

4951 International Drive, Orlando; tel: 407-352-9600; www.primeoutlets.com; daily 10am–9pm; I-Ride: mainline; map p.136 B3

There are currently over 100 stores in this mall, and an expansion is planned for 2008. Factory outlets include Nike, Gap, Adidas, Reebok, Tommy Hilfiger, and Neiman Marcus.

Winter Park Village

510 North Orlando Avenue, Winter Park; tel: 407-571-2700; www.shopwinterparkvillage.net; Mon–Sat 10am–7pm, Sun noon–5pm, restaurants and cinema open later; Link: 1, 2, 9; map p.135 D4

Several large anchor stores and the Regal Cinema border Winter Park Village's small, walkable "main street", with a collection of smaller independent shops and familiar chains. Like everything else in Winter Park, the place feels spacious, calm, and high-class. This town does not do discount malls. There are also several places to eat or drink here.

Independent Shops

MENSWEAR

John Craig

Winter Park: 132 Park Avenue South; tel: 407-629-7944; www.johncraigclothier; Mon–Sat 10am–6pm, Sun noon–5pm; map p.30

J.W. Marriott Grande Lakes: 4040 Central Florida Parkway Orlando; tel: 407-393-3747; daily 9am–7pm

Recently named one of the top 100 independent men's retailers in the US by *Esquire* magazine, this upscale store offers everything from made-to-measure suits and shirts to off-the-rack designers such as Zanella and David Chu.

BEACHGEAR

Ron Jon Surf Shop

4151 North Atlantic Avenue, Cocoa Beach; tel: 321-799 8888; daily 24 hours

A neon-lit palace devoted to bikinis, boogie boards, surfboards, scuba equipment, and other beach and surf gear. Famous surfers occasionally drop in for autograph sessions; scuba diving and surfing lessons are also available.

Below: subtle souvenirs make the best presents.

Sport

Whether you're a couch jockey or a true athlete, Orlando has more than enough sports-related activities to keep you happy, and there is hardly a hotel that doesn't offer amenities meant to keep their guests fit. Balmy year-round weather makes the area a natural choice for golfers, fishermen, tennis players, and other outdoorsy types. For those desperate to catch a wave, Cocoa Beach is only about an hour's drive away. The Orlando Magic may be the only fully professional sports team in the area, but each spring brings half of the Major League baseball teams to the state for their spring training games.

Baseball

Baseball fans can cheer for the Class AA Orlando Rays (www.orlandorays.com) at Disney's Wide World of Sports. Tickets are about $10. The Disney complex is also home to the Atlanta Braves' spring training camp, as well as a wide range of professional and amateur competitions. Check www.disneysports.com for a schedule of upcoming events.

Basketball

The Orlando Magic is the city's professional basketball team. They play at the Amway Arena. The season begins in September and runs through May. Call the box office (tel: 407-849-2020) for information and tickets.

Boating, Canoeing, and Water-skiing

The Walt Disney World Resort has a web of waterways connecting lakes large and small, and almost all of its resorts are on a lake or canal, with their own landing places or marinas. Dozens of different types of pleasure craft can be rented.

For sailing, conditions are best at two big lakes (Seven Seas Lagoon and Bay Lake at the Magic Kingdom resorts). Single hulls and catamarans are available at several Disney resort hotels. The same locations also have speedboats, drivers, and all the equipment necessary for water-skiing.

The canals around Fort Wilderness are good for canoeing, and you can take pedal boats on the lakes. If you prefer a motor to do the work, take a mini-speedboat, a gentler motorized raft, or rubber boat.

Outside the Walt Disney World Resort, several resort hotels have lakes and watersports opportunities, or check with your hotel guest services desk.

Fishing

Fish flourish in Florida's many lakes and canals thanks to

> Golf plays such a big role in Orlando's sporting scene, we've to devoted an entire chapter to it. For more information *see Golf, p.70–3*.

careful stocking and strict environmental policies. Guests at the Walt Disney World Resort are usually surprised to find that fishing is allowed from the shores at Fort Wilderness (but it is, of course, carefully controlled).

In addition, organized fishing expeditions leave daily from Bay Lake, starting off at 8am and in late morning and mid-afternoon. Reservations are required and the cost is quite high, but chances are good that you'll catch sizeable bass. Tackle, bait, and refreshments are provided.

Outside the Walt Disney World Resort, Florida's freshwater lakes and rivers are abundant. Try Lake Tohopekaliga (or Toho) in Kissimmee.

Rodeo

Kissimmee Rodeo
958 South Hoagland Boulevard, Kissimmee; tel: 407-933 0020; www.ksarodeo.com; Fri 8pm; admission charge; map p.18
Not so long ago, Kissimmee was one of the country's largest cattle-ranching areas, and folks around here like to

Left: Kissimmee's rodeo still attracts big crowds.

Central Florida YMCA Aquatic and Family Center

8422 International Drive, Orlando; tel: 407-363-1911; www.centralfloridaymca.org; Mon–Fri 6am–9pm, Sat 8am–5pm, Sun 12pm–4pm; admission charge; I-Ride: mainline; map p.136 A2

This Olympic-standard aquatic center is handily located on I-Drive for any swimmers craving a lengthier lap than most hotel pools offer. There are also t'ai chi and yoga courses, and racquetball.

celebrate the fact most weeks by taking part in a little friendly roping and riding. You'll see bareback riding, bull riding, bronco busting, and calf roping, as well as a calf scramble, in which kids from the audience chase a herd of young dogies. Concession stands sell cowboy hats and hot dogs, burgers, hot chocolate, and drinks.

If it's the real thing you're after, try to time your visit to Orlando for the Fourth of July, when the annual Silver Spurs Rodeo attracts professional rodeo riders from all over the United States.

Swimming and Surfing

Apart from the water parks, every resort and hotel in the Walt Disney World Resort has at least one pool. Many are imaginatively themed around ruined pirate forts, beached ships, grottoes, and mountains, and have fun slides for the children.

Then there are the beaches. The Walt Disney World Resort may be an hour's drive from the sea, but the lakeside resorts have fine,

white sandy shores, shady trees, lounge chairs, and cabanas – and the lake water is pure and clean. Lifeguards are on duty (if not, there will be a sign notifying you of their absence). Disney hotels' pools or beaches are open only to guests staying at Disneyowned accommodations, but many other resort hotels have excellent facilities, and most budget hotels or motels will have some sort of pool.

Outside the Walt Disney World Resort, Cocoa Beach, south of Cape Canaveral, has a fine beach with yearly surfing championships.

Tennis

More than two dozen tennis courts are scattered around the Walt Disney World Resort – at the Grand Floridian, Contemporary, and Fort Wilderness resorts; between the Walt Disney World Swan and Walt Disney World Dolphin, and at the Yacht and Beach clubs. If you want to improve your strokes, sign up for lessons with the pros at one of several Disney resorts. Outside the Walt Disney World Resort, the big hotels and country clubs all have courts.

Below: Cocoa Beach is of the east coast's premier surfing locations.

117

Themed Attractions

When you want to get away from it all, what more could you ask for than a vacation from reality? Whether it's watching lethargic alligators suddenly jump for their lunch, seeing first-hand freakery at Ripley's Believe It or Not!, or getting consumed in a virtual world, things are not always what they seem in Orlando. And with the weather so often hot, it should be no surprise that healthy competition exists between water parks, two of which are owned by Disney, inviting guests to come in, cool off, and get soaked.

Classic Florida

Gatorland

14501 South Orange Blossom Trail, Orlando; tel: 407-855-5496 or 800-393-JAWS; www.gatorland.com; daily 9am–5pm; admission charge; Link: 4; map p.18

Opened in 1949 by Kissimmee cattle rancher Owen Godwin, this 55-acre combination 'gator farm, exotic zoo, and wetlands is still the best – or at least the safest – place to have your Orlando alligator experience. This working 'gator farm sends about 1,000 'gators to market each week.

You can sample the taste of alligator meat in one of the restaurants, but don't miss classic entertainments like the **Gator Jumparoo Show**, where the critters jump for their dinner, and the **Gator Wrestling Show**, popular since Bunk Baxter first jumped astride a 'gator and opened its mouth for inspection in Downtown Orlando in the late 1800s.

These days, Gatorland uses more than half a century of experience with alligators to promote a strong conservation message (well, except when you

are eating them). It also works with the University of Florida on alligator research. And the Gator Night Shine program lets you explore the swampy walkways at night with nothing but a flashlight – a chance to experience the fear Florida's first settlers must have felt come nightfall.

Ripley's Believe It or Not!

8201 International Drive, Orlando; tel: 407-363-4418; www.ripleysorlando.com; daily 9am–1am, last ticket at midnight; admission charge; I-Ride: mainline; map p.136 A2

Below: memories of Old Florida at Gatorland.

Left: this is not a stunt show, here the danger is real.

wheels from the moon rover. One of the highlights is the state-of-the-art Simulator Station interactive area, where visitors can experience firsthand a variety of astronaut-training devices. Among them is a G-force centrifuge that creates the sensation of gravity four times that on Earth, a moon-walk simulator, and a shuttle simulator that allows visitors to test their piloting skills. Special activities are arranged for viewing shuttle launches, and astronauts occasionally drop by for a visit.

If you're in the mood for a walk on the weird side, head to one of I-Drive's most memorable buildings: an ornate Italian villa sliding into a Florida sinkhole. Newspaper cartoonist Robert Ripley had a taste for natural and manmade oddities, and made a fortune collecting bizarre artifacts from 198 countries. Prepare to be equally grossed out and intrigued by such exhibits as a two-headed calf, a Mona Lisa recreated in small squares of toasted bread, and a three-quarter-scale Rolls-Royce crafted from matchsticks. The topsy-turvy theme is carried through in skewed rooms, where things seem to roll uphill, and a disorienting catwalk, which appears to be stationary but is really moving.

U.S. Astronaut Hall of Fame
6225 Vectorspace Boulevard, Titusville; tel: 321-269-6100; daily 9am–5pm; admission charge, included in Kennedy

Space Center admission charge; map p.32
"[T]he surface was beautiful, beautiful… Magnificent desolation." So wrote Buzz Aldrin in a 1972 letter describing how it felt to walk on the moon. The document, on exhibit here, is just one artifact among thousands in this collection that tells the story of the American experience in space. But there's a lot more here, including a Mercury trainee capsule, the command module from Apollo 14, and

Fairground Attractions

Fun Spot Action Park
5551 Del Verde Way, Orlando; tel: 407-363-3867; www.funspot.com; hours vary with later opening times on Fri and Sat evenings; admission charge; I-Ride: mainline; map p.136 B2
Four twisting, multilevel tracks make this one of the best go-cart speedways in Orlando (try the 1,375ft, three-level QuadHelix for real thrills), and there are also bumper-car rides and other fairground attractions. For a

Right: the command module from Apollo 14.

Above: the upside-down eye-catcher that is Wonderworks.

change of pace, climb aboard the 101ft-high Ferris wheel for panoramic views of I-Drive and Universal Orlando. There is also a 10,000sq-ft video-game arcade.

Magical Midway
7001 International Drive, Orlando; tel: 407-370-5353; www.magicalmidway.com; Mon–Thur 2–10pm, Fri 2pm–midnight, Sat 10am–midnight, Sun 10am–10pm; admission charge; I-Ride: mainline; map p.136 A2

Owned by the same company that created Wonder-Works in order to compete with Ripley's Believe It or Not!, this park's obvious rival is Fun Spot, though its go-cart tracks are not nearly as well designed and unique. However, the price is nearly $10 cheaper.

Gamers' Heaven and Digital Dreams

DisneyQuest
Downtown Disney, Westside; tel: 407-828-4600; admission charge; map p.139 C2

What do you get when you compress all the thrills of a theme park into a five-story building? Well, something like DisneyQuest, a high-tech pleasure dome packed with simulator rides and souped-

up video games in a wavy, aquamarine building. Like a real theme park, DisneyQuest is divided into distinct areas, each spread over several levels connected by a labyrinth of elevators (known here as cyberlators), ramps, and twisting slides. Also like a real theme park, admission isn't cheap, and afternoon crowds can be extremely thick.

Wonderworks
9067 International Drive, Orlando; tel: 407-351-8800; www.wonderworksonline.com; daily 9am–midnight; admission charge; I-Ride: mainline; map p.136 A1

If illusions and tilted buildings are your thing, don't miss WonderWorks, next to Pointe Orlando. In typical Orlando one-upmanship, the three-story WonderWorks tops Ripley's by featuring a subsiding neoclassical building that is also upside down. Inside, it's a gamer's heaven, with more than 100 games, science-museum-style hands-on experiments that teach physics, and the world's largest laser tag game. Other attractions let you design and ride your own virtual roller coaster, experience an earthquake, or take part in virtual-reality war.

Religious Centers

Holy Land Experience
4655 Vineland Road, exit 31 on I-4, Orlando; tel: 407-367 2065; www.theholylandexperience.com; Mon–Thur 10am–7pm, Fri–Sat 9am–9pm, Sun noon–7pm; Link: 303; map p.136 B4

No matter where you stand on the novelty of a Christian theme park, this $16 million, 15-acre "Living Biblical Museum" is undeniably well executed and uses effective multimedia presentations to interpret the roots of Christianity, albeit from a distinctly partial point of view.

The park reflects the combined efforts of Islands of Adventure design firm ITEC Entertainment and founder Marvin Rosenthal, a Jewish-born Baptist minister. Rosenthal's motives for creating the park have been

All water parks are cleverly designed and well landscaped, and their slides can be thrilling. They are also usually crowded, as they make popular places to cool off during a scorching Florida afternoon. Like the theme parks, the trick to beating the crowds is to arrive about 30–45 minutes before opening and make a beeline to the most popular slides. By noon on a hot day, the queues can be prohibitively long and the pools unpleasantly mobbed. Another option is to arrive in the late afternoon – say 4–5pm – after the early birds have pooped out and gone home. Consider, too, that frequent electrical storms in summer will cause the water parks to close. A long storm can work in your favor, however, since some guests will get discouraged and return to their hotels. Bring a towel, sunscreen, snacks, and enough cash to last you the day.

Above: an actor at Holy Land Experience.

questioned since the project was announced in 1993. None of this seems to bother Christian groups, though, who have made up the vast majority of visitors since the park opened in February 2001.

The core of the Holy Land Experience is a re-creation of the city of Jerusalem between 1450 BC and AD 66 that includes the world's largest scale model of the Calvary Garden Tomb, the Wilderness Tabernacle, and the Qumran Dead Sea Caves. A scriptorium houses one of the world's largest private collections of original biblical manuscripts and books. Live shows, including **Behold the Lamb, Passion Drama**, often take place in the Plaza of the Nations on the steps of the Temple of the Great King.
SEE ALSO LIVE SHOWS, P.79

WordSpring Discovery Center
11221 John Wycliffe Boulevard, Orlando; tel: 407-852-3626; www.wordspringdiscovery center.com; Mon–Fri 9am–4pm, Sat 10am–4pm

The WordSpring Discovery Center is a fascinating explanation of the work of the Wycliffe Bible Translators. Linguists, as well as those visiting for spiritual reasons, will find the

exhibits on language learning and acquisition intriguing. Wycliffe's goal is to translate the Bible into every language in the world. In the process, representatives located in some of the world's remotest areas are preserving some of the world's most endangered languages, and, in some cases, they are creating written languages for people who currently only communicate via the spoken word.

Thrills and Spills
Richard Petty Driving Experience
3450 North World Drive, Lake Buena Vista; tel: 407-934-7639; www.1800bepetty.com; see website for schedule; Link: 50, 56; map p.138 A3

While most attractions in Orlando appeal to the whole family, this is strictly for the big boy racers. If you've always wanted to drive a souped-up, 630-horsepower Pontiac Grand Prix at 125mph, this NASCAR-affiliated racing school is the place. Choices range from a three-lap shotgun ride with a professional driver to an intensive two-day program that includes exercises in side-by-side driving and a

final duel on the speedway between student and pro.
Skyventure
6805 Visitors Circle, off International Drive, Orlando; tel: 407-903-1150; www.skyventure orlando.com; Sun–Thur 11.30am–9pm, Fri and Sat 11.30am–10pm; admission charge; I-Ride: mainline; map p.136 A2

This unique attraction uses an inverted wind tunnel to generate enough upward force to allow you to "fly" above it. The experience lasts for an hour, but only a couple of minutes of this time is spent flying, making this one of the most expensive experiences in Orlando.

Water Parks
Aquatica
International Drive; tel: 407-351-3600; www.aquaticaby seaworld; map p.139 E4

Due to open in 2008, Aquatica will be a traditional water park with slides, a lazy river and other such rides. The unique attraction will be a clear tube slide that goes through a dolphin-filled aquarium. See the website for the latest details.
Discovery Cove
Discovery Cove Way, Orlando; tel: 407-370-1280;

Below: the WordSpring Discovery Center explores language and faith around the world.

Above: I-Drive's most popular place to cool off.

www.discoverycove.com; daily 9am–5.30pm; Link: 8, 43; map p.139 E4

This free-standing, all-inclusive resort-style park is across the road from Sea-World. Up to 1,000 lucky guests a day arrive at the attractive, thatch-roofed tiki entrance to register for a day of sunbathing, swimming, interacting with tropical animals, and – the highlight – swimming with a dolphin.

Imported sandy beaches, deckchairs, cabanas, and refreshment stands surround the cool, saltwater Coral Reef, which has been stocked with stingrays and 6,000 tropical fish, as well as glassed-in sharks, a grouper, and a moray eel. Nervous youngsters (and adults) can enjoy the stingray experience in a baby stingray pool adjoining the Coral Reef.

But if that's too much for some – as it may well be – plan on floating around the park in the warm, freshwater Lazy River, passing waterfalls and submerged ruins. The river will lead you to the Aviary, a hugely popular spot, where staff members answer questions and hand you cups of food for the toucans, ibises, sun conures, guinea fowl, and even a tiny muntjac deer. A substantial gourmet lunch is included in the fee.

While it's possible to enjoy all this and more by signing up for the less expensive Non-Dolphin Swim Package, you'll probably kick yourself later if you don't take the opportunity to get into the water with one of the 30 dolphins. You can't change your mind when you arrive; the park is sold to capacity almost every day, and there are few last-minute cancellations. If you haven't made reservations, you're out of luck.

Included in the **Dolphin Swim Package** is a 30-minute session interacting with a dolphin and two trainers in groups of no more than six people. Dolphin swims

take place at specific time slots all day. You will be given your time when you arrive at the park and assigned a special cabana, where you will receive an orientation before getting into the water. The skill of the trainers makes this a very safe experience, and great care is taken to give each guest ample one-on-one dolphin time. You'll get a chance to try out hand signals to get your dolphin to roll, wave flippers, exchange kisses, and tow you along. And that, everyone seems to agree, is an experience that is almost priceless.

Disney's Blizzard Beach
1500 West Buena Vista Boulevard, Bay Lake; tel: 407-939-7812; hours vary; map p.138 B1

This is Disney's newest and largest water park, and the one with the most bizarre concept. At its center is **Mount Gushmore**, a 90ft peak serviced by what may be the state's only ski lift (there are also stairs and a gondola for disabled guests). At the top, guests choose among an assortment of routes to ride back down. The most exciting, the **Summit Plummet**, actually begins on a platform 30ft above the mountaintop. Other attractions suit quieter pursuits such as white-water rafting or floating down the lazy river. For kids, **Tike's Peak** and the **Ski Patrol Training Camp** have tubes, body slides, and a bungee cord slide. Blizzard Beach is also home to **Disney's Winter Summerland Miniature Golf**, with two elaborately designed 18-hole courses.

Above: the once-in-a-lifetime experience of Discovery Cove.

Disney's Typhoon Lagoon
1195 East Buena Vista Drive,
Lake Buena Vista; tel: 407-939-7812; hours vary; map p.139 C2
Typhoon Lagoon, we are led to believe, is the water-logged remains of a tropical resort drowned by a hurricane. In the center of the park is the **Surf Pool**, which generates waves more than 5ft tall, high enough for the surfing competitions that are held here. Rising above this scene is the summit of the 85ft-high **Mount Mayday**, crowned with the wreckage of *Miss Tilly*, a washed-up trawler.

The action is a bit tamer here than at Blizzard Beach, but not by much. You can lounge on a sandy beach, frolic in the waves, and take a relaxing 45-minute float trip through rainforest grottoes and waterfalls. At **Shark Reef**, you get a brief snorkeling lesson, then fin around a sunken tanker accompanied by tropical fish and real (friendly) sharks. This is one adventure you want to do just after the park opens. By midday, the lines are too long and the tank too crowded to be much fun.

There's no lack of high-speed slides, either. Daredevils shoot the rapids, careen through caves, and fly down a trio of 214ft speed slides at **Humunga Kowabunga**. The thrills are toned down at **Ketchakiddee Creek**, designed especially for children aged two to six.

Wet'n Wild
6200 International Drive,
Orlando; tel: 407-351-9453;
www.wetnwildorlando.com; see website for hours; admission charge; I-Ride: mainline; map p.136 A2

Near Universal Studios, a massive tower holds three rides: **Mach 5**, a spiraling flume; **The Blast**, their newest ride, which is your standard raft ride with added sound effects and water cannons that ensure you get soaked; and **The Flyer**, a fast drop in a raft that offers the park's biggest thrills. The Surge, in a separate tower, offers another hairy ride, as your raft screams down a banked tube some five stories high. Small children have their own fun in the sun: a kiddie pool and a pint-size multilevel water play area that includes water cannons, slides, the mini **Surf Lagoon** wave pool, and a **Lazy River** that takes you through Florida's past. The water at Wet'n Wild is heated, and the park is open year-round, though you'll find the winter months quite chilly.

Below: Disney's water parks are as well crafted as their other theme parks.

Thrill Rides

For certain tourists the accumulated miles of steel track at Orlando's theme parks are not to be feared but challenged. Below we list the best thrill rides at each park. Some, relatively speaking, are a doddle, where others will scare the life out of even the most seasoned riders. If you are a real aficionado and want to ride attractions several times, take advantage of single-rider lines and the FASTPASS and Express options available at Disney and Universal, respectively. For families traveling with children too short to enjoy a ride, most will have a parent swap station allowing one parent to ride while the other looks after the child.

Magic Kingdom

Splash Mountain
Frontierland; height requirement: 40in; FASTPASS

This down-home log ride features characters out of the Brer Rabbit children's story. For most of the ride this seems little more than a trumped-up dark ride, and then you come to the end: a five-story drop that guarantees to get you wet.

Big Thunder Mountain Railroad
Frontierland; height requirement: 40in; FASTPASS

While no self-respecting thrill-seeker would call this a proper thrill ride, it is a good stepping stone for those who have just graduated from the kiddie coasters or are trying to gain courage for Space Mountain. The runaway train never exceeds 40mph during its twisting and turning journey.

Space Mountain
Tomorrowland; height requirement: 44in; FASTPASS

For many, this is the only true thrill ride in the Magic Kingdom, and with a maximum speed of just under 30mph, it is quite tame in comparison to more recent coasters built elsewhere. It is still a classic, though, and the FASTPASSes for this ride through the darkness of space run out by midday, so get one quick if you plan to ride it at all.

Epcot

Mission: SPACE
Future World; height requirement: 44in; FASTPASS

This is the most sophisticated motion simulator in Orlando. Strapped into your spaceship's cockpit, the G-forces of take-off are recreated using an enormous centrifuge which slows down just as you exit the Earth's orbit, giving you a temporary feeling of weightlessness. The views of your home planet are equally serene, but don't think the ride is over just yet – you also have to land. This ride is so intense that Disney has recently created a "light" version that does not include the centrifugal force. To our knowledge this is still the only thrill ride in Orlando to come with a sick bag.

Below: be sure to leave your witch's broom in a locker.

Left: you'll never look at mummies the same again.

Some thrills come in small packages, and little ones may use these attractions to test their limits in preparation for riding the more serious thrill rides later.

Below are listed some remedial thrill rides, equally guaranteed to get a response of approval from under-8s and a sigh of boredom from teenagers:

High in the sky but only round and around, kids love the heights and slow comfort of hub-and-spoke classics such as the Magic Carpets of Aladdin (Adventureland, Magic Kingdom), Dumbo's Flying Elephant (Fantasyland, Magic Kingdom), Astro Orbiter (Tomorrowland, Magic Kingdom), TriceraTop Spin (DinoLand U.S.A., Animal Kingdom), and One Fish, Two Fish, Red Fish, Blue Fish (Seuss Landing, Islands of Adventure). Pteranodon Flyers (Jurassic Park, Islands of Adventure) is equally popular for its eye-in-the-sky orientation.

Spinning until sick is another favorite little-people pastime. It's amazing how much longer a child can withstand these rides than their gullible parents: Mad Tea Party (Fantasyland, Magic Kingdom) and Storm Force Accelatron (Marvel Super Hero Island, Islands of Adventure).

And finally, little tikes' coasters are great introductions to the steel-track bohemiths: Barnstormer at Goofy's Wiseacre Farm (height requirement: 35in, Mickey's Toontown Fair, Magic Kingdom), Woody Woodpecker's Nuthouse Coaster (height requirement: 36in, Woody Woodpecker's Kidzone, Universal Studios).

Test Track

Future World; height requirement: 40in; FASTPASS

For years this re-creation of automobile-testing procedures was the only thing approaching a thrill ride in Epcot. The ride does show its age now and is mild in comparison to other rides in the resort, but the finale, which includes banked turns at over 60mph, is a classic. The ride has notoriously long lines, though, so use your FASTPASS or join the single-rider queue.

Animal Kingdom

DINOSAUR

DinoLand U.S.A; height requirement: 40in; FASTPASS

What begins as a gentle dark ride ends with roller coaster-like drops and spins. This is ideal for those wanting thrills, but who may be a bit too young (or short) for Expedition Everest.

Expedition Everest

Asia; height requirement: 44in; FASTPASS

Disney's newest thrill ride feels like a decrepit mountain train scaling its way up the side of the world's tallest peak, and includes a steep backward drop when you come to the "end of the track." As if that weren't enough to frighten you, there is always the chance that the Yeti might surprise you as well.

Hollywood Studios

Rock 'n' Roller Coaster Starring Aerosmith

Sunset Boulevard; height requirement: 48in; FASTPASS

Though this coaster's design is enclosed, this is no Space Mountain. It begins with a 0–60mph acceleration that exerts over 4Gs on the riders. This is then followed by a loop, a roll, and a corkscrew. As if that were not enough, the entire ride is synchronized to a custom-made Aerosmith soundtrack. Lightweights need not apply.

The Twilight Zone Tower of Terror

Sunset Boulevard; height requirement: 40in; FASTPASS

The basis of this ride is a simple lift-and-drop amusement ride, but Disney Imagineers have done their best to make it even scarier. After checking in to the decrepit hotel, Rod Sterling from the *Twilight Zone* series is your guide through a series of disorientating exhibits that precede a random series of drops and lifts from the 13-storey building.

Universal Studios

Revenge of the Mummy
New York; height requirement: 48in; Express

Billed as a psychological thrill ride, novice riders may find that they do need therapy after this journey through haunted Egypt. Mummy uses intense special effects and terrifying voices in an attempt to play with your mind. Be careful you don't get too relaxed at the beginning of the ride, when it seems little more than a very well-executed haunted house. That is only the beginning. The ride reaches speeds of up to 45mph and includes periods of total darkness.

Islands of Adventure

The Amazing Adventures of Spider Man

Marvel Super Hero Island; height requirement: 40in; Express

This ride combines the finest elements of theme-park design. The track is classic dark-ride material enhanced by the use of 3-D technology, and the car you board is a fully maneuverable motion simulator. These elements combine to convince you that you are flying over the city, and it's impossible to believe that you are standing still at the finale.

Dueling Dragons
Lost Continent; height requirement: 54in; Express

Three elements make this one of the best rides in the southeast. First, it's an inverted coaster. This means the cars attach to the track overhead, while your legs dangle freely below (and sometimes above). Next, it's not merely one coaster, but two. Fire Dragon and Ice Dragon ride on intertwining tracks devilishly engineered for several near misses. Last, the attraction is elaborately themed, with a long, long

> A computer system monitors the trains in order to minimize the flyby distance between the trains – and maximize the terror.

queuing area that passes through castle ruins ostensibly destroyed by the feuding dragons. Merlin the Magician appears and warns you to turn back before it's too late, and tells the story of the legendary beasts – Pyrrock and Blizzrock – and the ill-fated knights whose charred and frozen remains are strewn about the place.

Fire is slightly faster – 60mph compared to Ice's 55mph – and has a bit more snap, but both deliver multiple loops, corkscrews, rolls, and up to 5Gs. Expect an extremely long wait for all but the earliest and latest few rides; the wait is even longer if you are one of those peculiar gluttons for punishment who elect to sit in the front cars. Do yourself a favor and get a Universal Express ticket.

Right: SeaWorld's Kraken may be surrounded by cuddly animals, but it's a beast.

Flying Unicorn
Lost Continent; height requirement: 36in; Express

Children and others who aren't up to Dueling Dragons can take a spin on The Flying Unicorn. The queue moves fairly quickly, so you can ride two or three times while others take on the dragons.

Incredible Hulk Coaster
Marvel Super Hero Island; height requirement: 54in; Express

This is Orlando's most memorable thrill ride, and you could not go home and call yourself a thrill-seeker without riding this at least twice. The trip begins with a 0–40mph acceleration that takes all of two seconds and is followed by seven inversions, including a unique cobra roll, and a top speed of 67mph.

SeaWorld
Journey to Atlantis
Height requirement: 42in

A unique attraction that combines the thrills of a roller coaster with a water ride whose final 60ft soaking plunge is one of the steepest in the world. There's a storyline behind the ride having to do with the Lost Continent of Atlantis and a battle between the gods, but once your boat gets moving it's all secondary to the action. There's a barrage of lasers, holographs, and other special effects, and a rapid-fire succession of drops and dips, including two 60ft dives that will have your stomach doing somersaults. Expect to get drenched, especially in the front seats.

Left: Universal's most daring roller coaster.

The only drawback is the long waiting time, which can be as much as an hour during the busy season. Your best strategy is to ride early in the morning or late in the afternoon.

Kraken
Height requirement: 54in

This 150ft-high, floorless roller coaster, named after a legendary sea monster, will terrify the living daylights out of even seasoned riders. Raised seats allow your legs to dangle freely as this monster reaches speeds of 65mph, creating a G-force that keeps you glued to your seat during a three-and-a-half-minute ride involving seven inversions (including a cobra roll, vertical loop, and flat spin), underground passages, and a soaking in the eel-infested monster's lair.

Space Coast
Shuttle Launch Experience
Minimum height: 48in

Created shortly after Epcot's Mission: SPACE, this is a much tamer ride. The concept, however, is exactly the same: to let you feel just what the astronauts feel when a space shuttle is launched. The biggest difference between the two rides is that you do not feel the heavy G-forces here as there is no spinning involved. The pre-show here also pays more attention to what actually happens in a real shuttle launch, explaining the physics of getting into outer space. Compared to Orlando's other motion simulators, this ride is rather tame, allowing visitors who are not exactly fans of thrill rides to get a taste of what it takes to get into space.

127

Transportation

Getting to Orlando should be no problem, nor should getting around this sprawling metropolis, so long as you know how to drive. Major airlines from all over the world serve Orlando International Airport, and it is a main stop on Amtrak's east-coast line. Once you've left the airport, the city spreads out in an orderly fashion around the Interstate-4 corridor. The sprawling layout does have its disadvantages: distances between attractions at Disney and those in Winter Park are great, and there is hardly any efficient public transportation to ease the journey.

Getting There

BY AIR

Most major US and international carriers serve Orlando. Fare prices are competitive, so shop around before buying a ticket. A variety of discount fares and "package deals," which can significantly cut round-trip rates, are also available. Many scheduled services are supplemented by charter flights.

Orlando (McCoy) International Airport (code MCO) is 9 miles south of Downtown Orlando and about 25 miles from Walt Disney World Resort. Spacious, glittering, and constantly expanding, it has three terminals, with satellite gates reached by "peoplemover" shuttle trains. Disney characters often make appearances during the day.

A lot of package flights land at Sanford Airport, about 30 miles north of Orlando. During the busy summer months this small airport is utilized to cope with the large numbers of tourists, and lines at immigration can be long. Furthermore, the extra distance can be a costly inconvenience if you plan to use taxi or shuttle buses to reach Orlando.

> Security at airports since September 11, 2001, has become a serious matter indeed. As long as you give yourself plenty of time, remain patient, and take absolutely no chances, you should be fine. Ensure that you are not taking any sharp objects onto the plane with you. Along with obvious weapons such as knives or scissors, nail clippers, jewelry with spikes on it, and even tweezers may be confiscated. Arrive early enough to deal with all the random searches. Three hours should be the norm now. Also be prepared for searches that may be embarrassing and/or offensive. Unfortunately, not all staff protecting the airports are as courteous as they might be. Remain calm and don't take it personally: they are only doing their job. Keeping your cool will also get you through quicker and with fewer hassles.

Orlando International Airport
Tel: 407-825-2001
Sanford Airport
Tel: 407-585-4000

AIRLINES
Telephone numbers of major airlines serving Florida (numbers are US unless stated):
American
Tel: 800-433-7300
UK tel: 020-7365-0777
www.aa.com
British Airways
Tel: 800-247-9297
UK tel: 0870-850-9850
www.britishairways.com
Continental
Tel: 800-523-3273
UK tel: 0845-607-6760
www.continental.com
Delta
Tel: 800-241-4141
UK tel: 0845-600-0950
www.delta.com
Lufthansa
Tel: 800-645-3880
UK tel: 0871-945-9747
www.lufthansa.com
Southwest
Tel: 800-435-9792
www.southwest.com
United Airlines
Tel: 800-864-8331

Left: arriving at Epcot in style.

Getting Around

TO/FROM THE AIRPORTS

Taxis and less expensive shuttle minibuses run between the airports and Walt Disney World locations, International Drive, Downtown Orlando, Kissimmee, and Cocoa Beach. Some hotels operate free shuttle services to and from the airports; if you are on a package tour, airport transfers may be included. There's a public bus – Lynx no. 42 – to International Drive that departs every 30 minutes from 5.15am–12.15am.

PUBLIC TRANSPORTATION

Like most cities in the United States, public transportation exists in Orlando but offers only infrequent service and only to major destinations. Luckily, this is usually along the tourist route. If you are staying along I-Drive, in Kissimmee, or in Downtown Orlando, service is adequate to other major areas only. Ask your hotel which bus takes you where, though be prepared for odd responses – most concierges are never asked for bus information. Your best bet is to call the Lynx information line.

UK tel: 0845-844-4777
www.united.com
US Airways
Tel: 800-428-4322
www.usairways.com
Virgin Atlantic
Tel: 800-821-5438
UK tel: 0870-380-2007
www.virgin-atlantic.com

BY RAIL

Amtrak offers slow and leisurely service from America's Midwest, northeast, and south – and connecting service from points west – to certain Florida cities. There is daily service from New York City on the Silver Service. The Sunset Limited travels from Los Angeles via New Orleans. For those who want to take their car along, too, Amtrak offers an Auto Train service from Lorton, Virginia (near Washington, DC), to Sanford, Florida, near Orlando.

Amtrak services within Florida are not extensive, being most useful for destinations along the east coast and in parts of central Florida.
Amtrak
Tel: 800-872-7245
www.amtrak.com

BY ROAD

Greyhound provides bus services to Florida and all over the state. While some intercity bus services include many stops en route, making long distances seem interminable, there are also express buses which take in fewer stops.

Many bus terminals, including the one in Downtown Orlando, are in a dodgy area of town, so take care when traveling to or from stations.
Greyhound
Tel: 800-231-2222
www.greyhound.com

Below: take a nostalgic trip down International Drive.

Above: trams make the arduous journey from car to gate a bit quicker.

Additionally, the I-Ride Trolley goes up and down I-Drive and Universal Boulevard from 8am–10.30pm. A single fare is $1.50, but exact change is required. They will (graciously) accept $2 to get you on your way, but you won't receive any change.

Lynx
Tel: 407-841-5969
www.golynx.com
I-Ride Trolley
Tel: 866-243-7483
www.iridetrolley.com

DISNEY TRANSPORTATION
The Walt Disney World Resort transportation system is complex, as are the rules about who can use it. They include those staying at Disney accommodations, at the Plaza hotels, or those carrying four- or five-day passes. Additionally, those with Magic Kingdom tickets can use the monorail or ferry to get to its entrance.

Disney buses connect all areas within the Walt Disney World Resort. They all look the same, but have electronic destination displays in the window to identify them. Bus stops outside parks and resorts are clearly labeled. If in any doubt, ask the driver. He or she will ever-so-happily tell you where they're

going, in between wishing everyone a magical day as they board.

The Disney World Monorail links Disney's Magic Kingdom resorts with the Magic Kingdom and Epcot.

Ferries run between the Ticket & Transportation Center (TTC) and the Magic Kingdom; between the Contemporary Resort, Magic Kingdom, and Wilderness Lodge; and between the Swan, Dolphin, and Yacht and Beach Club, BoardWalk Inn, and Hollywood Studios, as well as connecting all Epcot resorts.

UNIVERSAL STUDIOS TRANSPORTATION
Like Disney, all of Universal's resorts are linked to the parks by free transportation. In this case, though, it's all boats that dock at the City-Walk lagoon.

TAXIS
Taxis are available in all the main tourist centers. They tend to be expensive, and you usually have to telephone in advance for pickup. Your hotel should call for you; otherwise, numbers are listed in the Yellow Pages. Don't stand by the side of the road and expect to hail a passing cab.

Driving
Driving is the most popular way to travel to and around Orlando. More than 20 million visitors enter the Sunshine State by car every year – about twice as many as those entering by plane. Unless you plan to remain within Disney World or Universal Orlando during your entire stay, a car is the most convenient way to get around. Bus, train, and taxi service is quite irregular, and slow to cover the vast distances between Disney World and the rest of Orlando.

CAR RENTAL
Renting a car is by far the easiest way to explore the Orlando area beyond Disney World and Universal, allowing you to zip quickly between the major parks, unless, of course, you encounter one of the many traffic jams that snarl the area's major roads. If possible, avoid driving the I-4 corridor during rush hour (7–10am and 4–7pm).

Most rental agencies require that you are at least 21 years old (sometimes 25), have a valid driver's license and a major credit card. Some will take a cash deposit in lieu of a credit card, but this might be as high as $500. Travelers from some foreign countries may need to produce an international driver's license from their own country.

If you happen to book your car online in another

Florida has some of the toughest laws in the US against driving under the influence of alcohol. The maximum level permitted is so small that you are advised to drink no alcohol at all if driving.

country, you must provide a foreign driver's license for the discounted fee to be honored when you pick up the car.

Visitors wishing to rent a car after arriving in Orlando will find rental offices at the airports, at Downtown locations, and even at some hotels. Rates are cheap by US and international standards, but you should shop around for the best rates and features. Local rental firms outside the airports are often less expensive than the national companies, and can be more convenient if you want a car only for a day or two. The cost of insurance is usually tacked on to the rental fee, so be sure to check insurance provisions before signing anything.

If you are traveling from overseas, it is normally cheaper to arrange car rental in advance. You should also check with your airline or travel agent for special package deals that include a car, since rental rates can be reduced by about 50 percent if you buy a so-called "fly-drive" deal. However, be wary of offers of "free" car rental, which do not include extras like tax and insurance.

Available rental vehicles range from modest economy cars to luxury convertibles and vans.

Be sure to check that your car-rental agreement includes Loss Damage Waiver (LDW), also known as Collision Damage Waiver (CDW). Without it, you will be liable for any damage done to your vehicle in the event of an accident, regardless of whether or not you were to blame. You are advised to pay for supplementary Liability Insurance on top of the standard third-party insur-

ance. Insurance and tax charges combined can add $35 to each day's rental.

CAR RENTAL AGENCIES

These rental agencies may be contacted within the US and from abroad:

Alamo
Tel: 800-462-5266
www.alamo.com
Avis
Tel: 800-331-1212
www.avis.com
UK tel: 0844-581-8181
www.avis.co.uk
Budget
Tel: 800-527-0700
UK tel: 01344-484-100
www.drivebudget.com
Dollar
Tel: 800-800-3665
UK tel: 0808-234-7524
www.dollar.com
Hertz
Tel: 800-654-3131
www.hertz.com
UK tel: 0870-844-8844
www.hertz.co.uk
National
Tel: 800-227-7368
UK tel: 0870-400-4581
www.nationalcar.com
Thrifty
Tel: 800-847-4389
www.thrifty.com

SPEED LIMITS

American states set their own speed limits. In Florida they are: 55–70mph on highways, 20–30mph in residential areas, 15mph near schools.

Limits change suddenly and for only short distances, so pay attention to signs. The Highway Patrol is good at enforcing limits, including minimum speeds: signs along interstates sometimes oblige motorists to drive at over 40mph.

MAPS

Most service stations and convenience stores sell maps. Florida tourist offices (including overseas) often distribute the Official Transportation Map of Florida, which has city plans, free of charge.

Parking

All theme parks provide extensive facilities for car parking. There is usually a charge, although at Disney parks it is free if you are staying at Disney-owned accommodations and display the card that you are given when you register. If you do have to pay a parking fee, keep the ticket, since it is valid at all parks for that day. Remember to make a careful note of the exact location where you leave your car. After a few days of parking in vast lots that all look the same, it's easy to become confused.

Below: an American classic.

Atlas

The following streetplan of greater Orlando makes it easy to find the attractions listed in our A–Z section. A selective index to streets and sights will help you find other locations throughout the city.

Map Legend

☰	Freeway	▭	Urban area
	Divided highway	† †	Cemetery
	} Main roads	⌐ ¬	National park boundary
	} Minor roads	✈	Airport
═	Footpath	⚐	Beach
▬	Railroad	🚌	Bus station
⌁	Monorail	🅿	Parking
▰	Noteable building	❶	Tourist information
▰	Park	★	Sight of interest
▰	Hotel	⚑	Statue / monument
▭	Non-urban area	✛	Hospital

p134   p135

p136   p137

p138   p139

EAGLE
NEST PARK

Lake
Richmond

McLeod Road

34th Street
35th Street
36th Street

Central
Florida Ballet

Holy Land
Experience

Borrow
Pit

Millenia Road

Mall at
Millenia

Conroy Road

THE
EAGLEWOOD
GOLF CLUB

CYPRESS
CREEK
COUNTRY
CLUB

Tropical
Lake

TURKEY
LAKE
PARK

Turkey
Lake

Florida's Turnpike – Ronald

Conroy Road

Middlebrook
Road

Conroy Road

McLeod Road

Mission Road

Vineland Road

John Young Parkway

423

Havassee Road

LAKE
CANE-
MARSHA
PARK

Lake
Cane

Portofino
Bay Hotel

Universal
Studios

Hard Rock
Hotel

Major Blvd

4 Prime
Outlets

Lake
Marsha

Universal
Orlando
Resort

CityWalk

Islands
of
Adventure

Royal
Pacific
Resort

Festival
Bay Mall

Oak Ridge Road

ORANGE
TREE
COUNTRY
CLUB

Hollywood Way

Four Points by Sheraton
Orlando Studio City

Skyventure

Fun Spot
Action Park

Wallace Road

Holiday
Inn Express

Wet'n Wild

Howard
Johnson
Universal
Gateway Inn

Vanguard Street

Spring
Lake

Magical Midway

Sandy Lake
Enclave Suites
at Orlando

Pirates Dinner Adventure

Destiny
Nightclub

Fairfield Inn
by Marriott

Sand Lake Rd

Sand Lake Road

Little
Sand Lake

Bofa Ristorante

Best of British
Sports Bar & Grill

Central Florida YMCA
Aquatic & Family Center

Wyndham Resort

Ripley's Believe It or Not!

Goodings Plaza

Sleuth's Mystery
Dinner Show

Castle DoubleTree Resort

Orlando/Orange County
Convention & Visitors Bureau

Big
Sand
Lake

WonderWorks

Ming Court

Gio Lounge Orlando

The Outta Control Magic
Comedy Dinner Show

Pointe
Orlando

The Peabody
Orlando

SHINGLE CREEK
GOLF CLUB

Rosen
Shingle
Creek

Convention
Center

Bee Line Expressway

Ritz Carlton Orlando
Grande Lakes ↓

D   E

Michigan St
Pineloch   Avenue   (527)
Osceola St

McLeod Road
(4)
33rd Street
Lake Catherine

35th
37th St
41st St
43rd St

Westmoreland Drive

Rio Grande Avenue

(17)

(92)

Lake Holden

Lake Pinelock

Sumerlin Ave

Lake Jennie Jewel

Krueger Street

Forrestal Ave

Orange Avenue

Texas Ave

Lake Buchanan

Holden Avenue

Honour Road

Lake Tyler

Holden Avenue

Gatlin   Avenue

CYPRESS GROVE PARK

Lake Gatlin

EDGEWOOD

Redman Street

Americana Boulevard

Texas Avenue

Rio Grande Ave

Duskin Ave
Rose Blvd
Wakulla Way

Oak Ridge Road

Lake Ellenor

Chippia Circle

Tomoka Drive

Rockwood Ave

Lake Jessamine

Mary Jess Road

Lake Mary

Oak Ridge Road

Winegard Rd

Doss Ave

Jason St

Pierce Ave

Anno Avenue

Dumont St

Lancaster Road

Lake Ellenor Drive

441

Lancaster Road

Chancery Lane

Jordan Avenue

Voltaire Drive

Winegard Road

Bay Lake

Premier Row
Directors Row

Viscount Row

Currency Drive

Southland Boulevard

Blossom Trail

Orange Blossom Trail

Lake Road

(482)

Sand   Lake   Road

Lake Conway

Oak Island Rd

Hoffner Ave

BELLE ISLE

Hoffner   Avenue

Randolph St

Hansel Avenue

Orange Avenue

Matchett Road

Lake Conway

Nela Ave

Seminole Dr

Lake Drive

Gordon Road

Perkins Road

Bear Head Lake

Stafford Drive

Lake Conway

Trentwood Boulevard
McCoy Road

(482)

(528)

Florida Mall

(528)

Bee Line Expressway

Jetport Drive

Orlando International Airport

SOUTHPORT PARK

Morning Drive
(17)
Lake Christie
(92)

Donald

Consulate Dr.

Regan

Principal Row

(441)

Turnpike

Landstreet Road

Bachman Road

Thorpe Road

Recyle Center Rd

Sidney Hayes Road

Avenue E St

Avenue C

Orange Avenue

Landstreet Road

Pine Street

3rd Street
4th Street

Boggy Creek Road

Great Sound Drive

Andros Place

Binnacle Way

4th St

Taft Vineland Road

0   500   1000   1500   2000yds

0   500   1000   1500   2000m

D   E

p134   p135
p136   p137
p138   p139

Index